KENNET

NO
TEARS

THE TRIUMPHANT LIFE OF DR. KENNY D

KENNETH N. DANIELS, PH.D.

NO TEARS

The Triumphant Life of Dr. Kenny D

Copyright © 2020 by Kenneth N. Daniels
a.k.a. Dr. Kenny D, Dr. Kenny N. Daniels, Dr. Ken Daniels, Kenneth Daniels

All rights reserved.

No Tears: The Triumphant Life of Dr. Kenny D is a work of non-fiction. Some names and identifying details have been changed to protect the privacy of the people involved.

This book or parts thereof may not be reproduced in any form, stored in any retrieval system, or transmitted in any form by any means—electronic, mechanical, photocopy, recording, or otherwise—without prior written permission of the publisher, except as provided by United States of America copyright law. For permission requests, contact the author at the email address below. *Special thanks to the New Brunswick Free Public Library for their reference support and online historical data services.*

ISBN: 9798596644302

For press and media inquiries or bulk orders, please contact the Daniels Foundation via email: info@daniels-foundation.org

Visit us online: www.daniels-foundation.org

Join us and subscribe to our weekly podcast on YouTube to always hear the latest on our empowerment and economic development initiatives.

The Rewards of Wisdom

My son, forget not my law, but let thine heart keep my commandments. For length of days and long life, and peace, shall they add to thee. Let not mercy and truth forsake thee; bind them about the neck; write them upon the table of thine heart. So shalt thou find favor and good understanding in the sight of God and man.

Psalm 3:1-4

DEDICATION

This book is dedicated to the memory of my Aunt Hazel O'Bryant, who cherished me with love and understanding of people from all walks of life.

I also dedicate this to my Uncle Cleveland, who was a wise man. But most of my achievements were inspired by my Dad, Henry Beechwood Daniels, and my mother, Gwendolyn Mozetta Daniels. My mom was valedictorian of her high school in Bordentown, New Jersey, and my father was one of the first Black principals in the state of New Jersey in New Brunswick. These achievements are a substantial part of my heritage and played a vital role in my formative development.

Dedication

Dad (left) and I (right).

My Dad, Henry Beechwood Daniels (top left) being a pioneer and honored for making history *(The Daily Home News, New Brunswick, New Jersey, August 1967).*

Dedication

My Dad, Henry Beechwood Daniels with our family, The Sunday Home News, New Brunswick, New Jersey, October 1967).

First row (front) from left to right: Leslie, Dwayne, Norma, Sam, Johnny, Marianne, and Kenny.

Second row (middle) from left to right: Donald, Cheryl, Sandra, Kim, Courtney, Ronald, Opal, Donna, Beverly, and Andrew.

Third row (back) from left to right: Charles, Essence, Eugene Clarence, Janet, Sheila, and Jeffrey.

Dedication

Taylor (my son) and I.

Kirsten (my daughter in the middle) before her video shoot with friends, Ryan (right) and Claire (left).

Dedication

Mrs. Jeffries (left) and my mom, Gwen Daniels (right).

Aunt Hazel and Uncle Cleveland.

CONTENTS

DEDICATION vii

FOREWORD xv

INTRODUCTION 1

Chapter 1

    DREAMS OF BLACK ECONOMIC DEVELOPMENT 3

Chapter 2

    THE FALL 7

Chapter 3

    ACCUSATIONS 11

Chapter 4

    EVIL SPIRITS CIRCLE 18

Chapter 5

    A SECOND CHANCE AT LIFE AND LOVE 22

Chapter 6

    THE RISE 25

Chapter 7

    MY FIRST LOVES 30

Chapter 8

    THE FORMATIVE YEARS 38

Chapter 9

    THE FIRST TEAR 47

Chapter 10

    MEETING MY WIFE 51

Chapter 11

    MY CHILDREN 64

Chapter 12
LOST SONS 83

Chapter 13
THE FAIRFIELD YEARS 90

Chapter 14
THE UCONN YEARS 108

Chapter 15
IVORY TOWER 121

Chapter 16
BLACK MAN ON BOARD 133

Chapter 17
ENAYA AND THE QURAN 145

Chapter 18
THE QUEEN OF QUEENS 161

Chapter 19
THE KIDNAPPING 169

Chapter 20
A ROCKY ROAD HOME 178

Chapter 21
A FINAL PERSPECTIVE 185
ACKNOWLEDGEMENTS 193
ABOUT THE AUTHOR 195

FOREWORD

If ever there was any doubt about the spirit of mere mortals to overcome great misfortunes, Ken Daniels' saga will forever lay these doubts to rest. Having survived a serious, largely undiagnosed illness, huge disappointments in both his personal and professional life, Ken has now resurfaced to not only put his own life back on track, but more importantly, the lives of countless disenfranchised Black children via the creation of the Daniels Foundation for Impact Investments and Development.

I first met Ken in the mid 1990's when I was an Adjunct within the finance department of Virginia Commonwealth University. At that time, he took me under his wing by educating me on how to most effectively conduct the learning experience of my mostly adult and part time students.

It did not take long for me to realize that Ken was seeking to make a greater contribution to society than only by being a tenured Professor at a major public university. With that in mind, I may have been instrumental in getting him appointed to the Boards of the Virginia State Treasury Board as well as to the Retirement System of the City of Richmond.

These appointments changed the way business was normally conducted at these Boards. Rubber Stamping went out the window and serious issues and questions were raised as to how, why, when, and where various issues were being managed. This at first may have been a negative as staff was used to getting their way before Ken's appointment. But now- ALL THESE QUESTIONS! However, with time, the senior management and staff began to appreciate the challenges that they were sure to face at all board meetings and actually began to look forward to them. "What will he ask us about this?"

Ken became what we would call in 2021, a disrupter.

While Ken Daniels, as of today, may not be a household name, his is a name one needs to listen to and more importantly, learn from.

GREG SCHNITZLER
Retired Portfolio Manager
State Treasury Department
Commonwealth of Virginia

INTRODUCTION

MY NAME IS KENNETH NOLAN DANIELS and I grew to be Dr. Kenneth N. Daniels, a Black Scholar and entrepreneur in the United States of America. My friends would describe me as a kind, compassionate person who is a fighter. I have been fighting all my life for my dignity and fighting the good fight for what is right and to be the best person or man I could become in this life. This memoir or story is about the fight in me and the fight for a good life. A purpose driven life with meaning. Many Black men can learn from this book but many people can read it and learn from my experiences to craft a positive message of hope. In this book I open up my life to be truthful about the bad experiences in my life and how I sought closure to the bad events without holding on to the pain. I tried to dig deep in my soul to convey the depth of the human mind and spirit to illustrate the depth of our character. As I went through this experiment of documenting my feelings and desires I was encouraged to write a manuscript of my experiences by an old friend.

I began writing this book as I exited New Jersey and started living a carefree life in Florida after the end of my marriage, and several climatic events in my life. I needed a fresh start and the warm weather of Florida agreed with my mind, body and soul. It also gave me another chance to reflect on the past several years of my life. The ample time led to a reflective mood and I started to appreciate my current path in life with more optimism and hope. Although the past events still had not been totally rectified they had a pattern of possible closure. It was during this time that I reflected on my street savviness from growing up in urban America which gave me an inner toughness to deal with the severe racism that I encountered during my life and professional career. Racism is an evil sin that has inflicted many wounds on many men regardless of their color or culture. Dealing with an unfair system regardless of where it originates is a challenge for the

Introduction

individual and for the society at large for it has many externalities or consequences for the individual and the society at large. In my story I illustrate that racism is not just a Black and White problem but a systemic problem of hatred that emanates from some surprising places. Although I believe that racism is a known ugly evil as a societal ill, I don't know if we can fully comprehend the depth of racism until we hear the many untold stories of its ugly contamination.

One positive externality that was produced by my life experiences with racism was the Daniels Foundation for Impact Investments and Development. You can learn more about the foundation at www.daniels-foundation.org. After a lengthy academic career it came to an abrupt end due to a physical illness. At the time the life event was pretty traumatic and played a role in the divorce from my partner of 30 years. The perfect storm of life events centered around the death of my father, the death of my dog, the retirement from my job, my marital divorce and the separation from kids and mother. As you can see it was quite a traumatic series of events that a lot of people can relate to in one way or another. I can tell you that all the events taught me a lot as a person. The events led me to my eventual destination and the creation of a purpose driven life along with the organization of the Daniels Foundation for Impact Investment and Development. The Foundation is a testimonial to the educational career of my father Henry Beechwood Daniels. My Dad was one of the first Black principles in the State of New Jersey. He spent his lifetime allowing talented urban students to achieve at a high level and compete in the marketplaces of America and the world. This role model motivated me to try and empower the next generation of urban learners of all colors and cultures but with a special affinity for Black children and Black culture given my heritage.

I hope you take the time to read this memoir and book as it has a message of hope, and aspirations along with continued educational and spiritual development for a wide audience and group of people. I thank you in advance for any time you spend reading my story and look forward to hearing about your experience with my story.

1

DREAMS OF BLACK ECONOMIC DEVELOPMENT

SOMETIME IN 2015, I would mysteriously start falling asleep at my office desk. I would close my eyes for just a second, and when I reopened my eyes, two or three hours would have elapsed in what seemed to me at the time, only the blink of an eye. While I was sleeping, I would have these vivid dreams which were detailed and seemed like some kind of premonition of things to come. In some of my dreams, I could see individual faces down to the very wrinkles or spots. I could also recall a smile or a peal of laughter. Some of the individuals I knew and some I didn't. However, it wasn't until one particular drive home that I came to realize I had developed a severe sleep disorder when I stopped at a stoplight with my car and the foot on the brake. Feeling extremely tired at the stoplight, I closed my eyes for a second as I drifted off to sleep. The next thing I heard was a banging sound on my car window and a police officer asking, "Are you okay?"

I responded, "I am fine, sir."

Looking me squarely in the eye, the officer said, "I have been watching you as you slept at the light."

Looking around at my surroundings, I asked in a bewildered voice, "I was sleeping? Really?"

He answered, "Yeah, really. Do you live nearby?"

"Yes," I answered, "Just up the road."

He said, "I can't give you a ticket because you didn't do anything wrong, but I will follow you home to make sure you get home safe."

I slowly drove up Sliding Hill Road to the Ashland home, relieved that the officer was kind enough to let me drive home. What had just happened?

After visiting the clinic at Virginia Commonwealth University, where I worked, I would later learn that I had narcolepsy, a sleep disorder. Before 2015, I had not had any type of sleep disorder, and then suddenly, things changed in 2015. I found my sleep disorder to be quite a challenge initially because I could not complete some work assignments as I would literally fall asleep on the job. More importantly, the slumbering generated by my narcoleptic attacks produced vivid dreams that would capture my imagination and give me ideas about life, work, and the way I should live my life.

One dream that I had changed the course of my life. The dream was about me starting a foundation focused on the economic development of Black communities in America's inner cities. Over the next two years, I used my experience in academia and research to develop the Daniels Foundation for Impact Investments and Development. The Foundation was born in July 2017. It was set up as a nonprofit organization to develop affordable housing and provide educational programs such as financial literacy and some after-school programs for sports or remedial skills development.

The Daniels Foundation for Impact Investments and Development is an act of faith in God and His promise that if I build it, He will provide the resources needed to achieve the organization's goals and objectives.

I compare the building of the Daniels Foundation as a kind of institutional Ark, similar to Noah building the ark in the bible. However, my goal here is to help urban communities of all color advance and evolve our institutions to be more sophisticated and responsive to the future's technological changes. The church is the most stable and advanced institution in the Black community, and it has evolved to be a hodge-podge institution that does everything from child-care to banking. Churches are essential, but their primary function should be pastoring the people, and I believe in faith in action. However, the next evolution of Black people must be an advancement of our economic and institutional development. Our community needs entrepreneurial individuals to focus on the community needs while also acquiring personal wealth and assets. Other ethnic groups, such as the Jews and Koreans, have emerged as a race and found common ground as a group, which has allowed them to advance economically. It is time that Black people commit to institutional and economic development as a critical component of our survival tactics for the next generation.

The mission of the Daniels Foundation for Impact Investments and Development is primarily about the people. My affinity for helping Black people because of our history is the driving factor for creating the Daniels Foundation for Impact Investments and Development. However, the Foundation will help anyone who wants to help themselves. Economic development is built upon a solid foundation of education and integrity. I credit my economic development to the educational aspiration instilled in me by my father, Henry Daniels. He was one of the first Black principals in the State of New Jersey. My father's economic development was inspired by his mother, Priscilla Cooper, who many called the Madame CJ Walker of Philadelphia. She attended the all-Black Apex trade school and learned cosmetology. She inspired a high educational attainment level in my father and his brother Arthur, who became a very accomplished jazz musician. My father attained and inspired a high level of education in his children. I also did the same with my children. Today, my daughter is pursuing a Ph.D. in Nursing. Educational aspiration is still available in the Black community through our public-school system and many charter schools across the nation. Still, the record is spotty on the factors that drive performance and educational excellence. Also, having integrity ensures that one's goals are aligned with the highest ethical standards.

Another area that must have continued discussion and debate is public school finances as any state system which relies on the property tax for the majority of public-school financing will continue to find that poor communities will struggle to be competitive over time. One reason why a poor community will struggle is the community's original economic endowment is drastically different, along with the cultural approach to education and its components of reading, writing, and math. For example, on average White households read more books to their children pre-school than the average Black family. It is also well documented that many minority children are not prepared for kindergarten and that a significant investment in pre-kindergarten educational programs would reap significant rewards in urban neighborhoods. These cultural norms lead to faster language development, which plays a role in word knowledge and educational development. Some scholars go so far as to claim language acquisition leads to advantages in the early stages of brain development, leading to significant advantages later in one's educational attainment. So, the Daniels Foundation for Impact Investments and Development seeks to supplement inner-city educational programs with after school programs and enhancement programs such as financial literacy and any Pre-K educational programs.

Finally, the Daniels Foundation for Impact Investments and Development seeks to inspire kids to compete through the arts and sports. Girls' sports will be a central focus of the Daniels Foundation as females in sports often get overlooked. Sports can be the hook that gets Black youth in the door of many community centers throughout the nation, which could be staffed with exemplary after-school programs focused on skills development. Arts is an underfunded school activity, and many minority youths have significant talent in the arts, which could spark an entrepreneurial boom in urban neighborhoods and tourism.

I would like a future where Black communities are prosperous, not just here in the USA but also in the Motherland. This is my dream and aspiration. Before I could achieve this dream, my life would take another dramatic turn in 2016, in what I would now describe in the next chapter, "The Fall."

THE FALL

I THOUGHT BEING DIAGNOSED with Narcolepsy was terrible, but that was only the beginning of some of the darkest periods in my life.

In 2016, I went on a business trip to South Africa. Before leaving Virginia, I went to a local pharmacy to get the required vaccinations. The proper vaccination was a two-part vaccination. I got the first part of the vaccination but not the second shot. All seemed well when I boarded the 15-hour flight to Cape Town. But all was not well on my return. I did not feel like myself, and I became increasingly lethargic. The sluggish feeling increased significantly over a month. Soon, I could barely get out of bed. A trip to my doctor revealed that my testosterone levels had fallen to an abnormally low level.

When my wife noticed the abrupt behavior change, she was initially supportive. This quickly changed. With each passing day, my body deteriorated, and my wife became more and more distant. The severity of my illness began to fill her with dread. Soon, she became more concerned about her well-being and started searching for the nearest exit. I was helpless at the lowest point in my life, and my partner of 30 years had decided to bail. I thought to myself at that time, wow! A man cannot even get sick in his own home in peace. With little regard for my well-being, my wife quickly used my illness as an opportunity to leave me and move most of her clothes out of the house over two weeks.

Only when I saw myself lying in bed in a childlike cocoon did I realize how far I had fallen. The former captain of the college basketball team was now a broken man. I had lost it all in the blink of an eye. With each passing day, the strength ebbed from my body. The lethargy that enveloped my physical body was slowly reaching my mind.

As I laid in the bed sick, I knew she was leaving and packing up. Every weekend for a month, she left me in the house, sick, by myself, and with no food. When she came back on Sunday or Monday after a long weekend, she would bring me a couple of McDonald's hamburgers. I never cried when she left.

I was not even angry. I had slowly acclimated to surviving on as little food as possible. I tried to convince myself that I was glad when she finally left. Truth be told, I was broken, lonely, and afraid of facing a future alone. I thought of all the Thanksgiving dinners and holidays we spent together as a family. The realization that it was over left me numb. I could not cry, or maybe I just refused to. Instead, I curled my legs into a fetal position and entered my cocoon, and refused to leave the bed.

I was in the house in Ashland all by myself, and no one was coming to save me. My kids were busy with their lives, and my friends and family were primarily in New Jersey. As I laid in my cocoon, I thought about every major decision I had made in my life. Maybe I deserve this. After all, I had been unfaithful. I was no angel, and I think I know what the last straw that pushed Janet over the edge was. I was bored at work and even a little bored at home with Janet and our sex life. In the act of desperation to spell loneliness, I joined a dating website to spell boredom. I joined as anonymous and primarily looked at the pictures of the beautiful women. One day I was looking at the numerous pictures on my phone in the bathroom, and I left my phone in the bathroom. Janet found my phone and the dating website. She was crushed, and I had let her down. Janet didn't speak with me for weeks, but eventually, we reconciled, and we moved forward. I loved her. She was not only my wife; she was my best friend. She was the mother of my children. But now, at my weakest hour, Janet had enough of me and had decided to leave. I couldn't wrap my brain around the cold, nonchalant way she abandoned me in my time of need.

Ironically, I didn't think of the dating website as cheating on my wife. It was just a distraction from the monotony of married life that had crept in over 30 years. I thought of myself as a happily married man, and I was looking forward to us being empty nesters. Unfortunately, my illness got in the way, and she had a different agenda. Two weeks after my daughter graduated from college in May 2016, my wife had completely moved all her clothes out of the house and had an apartment in the West End of Richmond. The betrayal was not only physical and emotional; it was also financial. In one last turn of the knife, she raided our joint bank account, leaving me a small amount. I assume she used the money to move on. Now my empty nest household turned into an empty house. From May 2016 to October 2016, I spent many lonely nights rethinking my life. I questioned the colleges I attended. I questioned the decisions I made on the basketball court, and I wished I had taken that shot at Princeton to win the game in 1982. I questioned my parenting of my son and daughter. I questioned my professional behavior and productivity. I also questioned my indiscretions during the marriage and felt a sense of remorse for my actions.

I beat myself up pretty good and had a long pity party. Then I realized that no one cared. Or probably a more accurate view is that my friends and family cared but had their own problems. It was during this pity party that I learned the power of the mind. I had a long time to think and to challenge myself. In retrospect, it was a great opportunity to get some perspective on my life and what was important. As I mentioned earlier, my illness was almost like a cocooning process, which made me a new man. During my fall from grace, my mind was hell-bent on seeing how far I could fall and see if I could recover. As I think back now, I know it seems like a stupid idea. But that is what I did. At one point in that haze, I thought of the maxim 'a mind is a powerful tool' and just as the mind can be programmed for success, it can also be programmed for failure and self-destruction. Every day in society we hear of individuals in despair who commit suicide. The pain of living can become so burdensome that a person thinks it is rational to take their own life. By the mercies of God, at no time during that dark period of my life did I contemplate suicide. I could never end my life without a good fight. I wanted to live. I wanted to love again. I wanted to work again. I wanted to find God in my life, and I realized I had to fight. But I instinctively knew I had a long journey ahead as I laid on the bed all alone.

My illness started a cocooning process the day my wife left me. I call it a cocoon because my illness was almost like a spiritual awakening and a rebirth of my soul. Almost immediately, I was on my own and vulnerable. My wife knew of my vulnerability and used my weakness to conveniently time her exit.

3

ACCUSATIONS

WHEN I FIRST MET JANET, I thought she was a sweet, innocent young woman who didn't have a bad bone in her body. I found it attractive that she was essentially a blank canvas that I could help fill in her voids with imprints of my hopes and desires. I had dreams. She had dreams. Check. I was smart. She was smart. Check. I had ambition. She had ambition. Check. I came from a solid middle-class family. Janet came from a middle-class family but was adopted. This was a mismatch and later blossomed into a major mistake I made in vetting my partner.

I have no strong opinion on adoption. However, I do believe when a person chooses to go the route of adoption, he or she should be prepared to make sacrifices. More importantly, the adopted child should be loved unconditionally. Unfortunately for Janet, this was not the case as her parents loved her sister more than her, and this was one of many challenging relationships Janet would have during her life. The rejection she received from her parents paled in comparison to the rejection she got from her biological parents. Janet's mother was Italian, and her father was a Black man. Janet never attempted to discover their identity during our relationship. But by God's hand, the Italian family would have nothing to do with the bastard child produced by the Black man. You see, in the 1940s and 1950s, Italian families had strong bonds and lineages that were Italian pure. Janet's existence threatened the purity of a traditional Italian family and was not permitted to contaminate the Italian bloodline. Her Italian mother was forced to put her up for adoption.

By the grace of God, Charles and Lillian Norman adopted Janet with unconditional love in their heart as their marriage was childless and Charles' traditional Caribbean mother was pressuring him to give her a grandchild. Initially, Janet entered the traditional Caribbean family culture with love and respect and a middle-class opportunity. She was first rejected and now unconditionally accepted. That all changed when Janet's sister, Helaine, was born. Now, the Normans had a biological child and an adopted child. Quickly, Helaine became the favorite, as told by Janet. She once said to me, "Helaine could do no wrong, and I had to be perfect."

Janet fell into a conditional love relationship with her father. It presumed that Janet would take care of him and the mother in exchange for acceptance and love. I witnessed the indentured relationship first-hand, and it sickened me to my stomach. How could parents be so cruel and filter their love unconditionally to one child but conditional to the other based on service? It happened so easily as Janet desired so much in her heart to please her father, the Tortola Black racist. Why would I label Mr. Norman such a harsh term? Well, he wasn't exactly nice to me as a father-in-law. He was quite mean to me. Every time I entered their house during our marriage, he would proclaim, "Here is the nigger boy from East Orange."

If the taunting stopped there, I probably would have forgiven my father- and mother-in-law, but the taunting would then proceed to the dinner table. Comments such as, "Ken, why do the niggers in Newark steal so much?"

A family chuckle would follow, with Janet sitting quietly, not daring to hush the Mrs. Norman who was Black. She was also very insensitive to me and called me a lazy nigger often, usually under a whisper. She would say, "Boy, you a lazy nigger."

I have no idea why my mother-in-law thought I was lazy. I was a tenured full professor in finance. These nigger name-calling sessions were often and frequent at Norman's home and even went on the road to our home or family holidays.

I can vividly remember one Thanksgiving holiday when I met a majority of Janet's family for a so-called turkey dinner. Little did I know that I would be the main turkey in a nigger name-calling session. Most of the insults came from Janet's cousin, Archie, a cop from Asbury Park. Archie was your typical light-skinned Caribbean man with blue eyes. There had been some race-mixing in the family as most of the Norman clan looked like Archie. The discussion started normally, "Ken, nice to see you."

Other family members included Tony and Albert Greenwood. Tony was a former FBI agent who now owns several McDonalds in Florida, and his brother Albert is the family underachiever. It was no secret that Albert didn't like the successful Tony. The first blow came when Archie said, "Ken, why don't the niggers up there comb their hair?"

I was shocked and replied, "What do you mean, Arch?"

He said, "You know the niggas keep a pick in their hair, but the niggas naps don't get picked."

Suddenly there was a peal of laughter from Tony. Albert and Mr. Norman had drifted into the nigger conversation.

Mr. Norman then piled on, "Yeah, Ken is our nigger boy from East Orange."

Archie couldn't wait and jump on the fresh meat of bigotry. "Oh, you from EO Ken," he said.

Staring the blue-eye Archie down, I said proudly, "Yeah, I am from EO."

Archie followed, "Yeah, the crime there is so high from the niggas stealing."

At this point, I had enough and left the room to see Janet. I said, "Jan, they believe I am a nigga from East Orange."

She responded, "Well, you are from East Orange, and South Jersey people don't think too highly of Blacks from EO or Newark."

I was floored. I was surrounded by Black bigotry, and it wasn't looking pretty. More importantly, I learned my wife was a closet racist against Black people and favored her Italian heritage over her Blackness.

The initial years of my marriage to Janet were challenging as she struggled professionally. As the only female Black engineer in a predominantly White civil engineering profession in the capital of the Confederacy, there was little kindness and even fewer opportunities for Black staff engineers. This rejection from her profession troubled Janet as she worked hard to become a good to a great engineer. She was targeted with hatred and bigotry that was shocking and unreal. The White male-dominated profession hated any advantage given to minorities. This just fueled the debate of affirmative action versus set-asides as a minority employment tool. The major court case on affirmative action is in Richmond, Virginia. Janet was intentionally alienated as a female Black engineer. She also felt disconnected and left out of any social norms of the profession. I encouraged Janet to not give in to the under-belly of the predominately White engineering profession but to fight back by starting her engineering firm. She followed my advice and started Daniels and Associates, the only female Black-owned engineering firm in Richmond. Virginia.

Although Janet was a good engineer, her firm initially struggled to gain traction, and I supported the family finances primarily with my University earnings and my summer teaching earnings. This trend would continue for the early years of Janet's firm development as the White male engineering firms used nasty business practices to hold her firm back, such as putting her work through much more rigorous review processes than the norm. Despite the professional rejection, Janet flourished as a woman in the early years of the firm's development. She was bright, beautiful, and tough. The industry hardened her into a professional fighter as she constantly battled racist attack after racist attack.

Little did I know that this hardened professional skill would be aimed at me during our divorce.

Eventually, Janet's firm, Daniels and Associates, broke out and became one of the more profitable minority firms in Richmond, Virginia. I was relieved as Janet could now contribute to the household finances. As Janet rose in stature, so did the Daniels family in the social settings of the old Confederate capital. Janet and I worked hard to be successful in Richmond, Virginia, and we succeeded in breaking down old norms of discrimination and rise into the Black Richmond social life.

Janet craved to go higher in the Black Richmond social life. I could care less and focused on my career. Janet, on the other hand, struggled with basic business concepts as she was not formally trained in the business. Besides, she made a mistake and hired an unprepared person to run her finances instead of the usual business practitioner. This was a mistake because Shelly stole over $100,000 from Janet's firm and created a cash flow problem for Janet's firm. Furthermore, Shelly was given the serious White privilege as she did no jail time and didn't have to pay back the stolen funds. Janet was extremely hurt by Shelly's rejection as she was at Shelly's wedding, and they were quite close, it seemed. I am saddened when I recall this episode of our Richmond life as Janet's life lost some innocence and the hardened Black female engineer became more desperate to achieve success.

Janet's desperation revealed itself to me in a shocking moment of her rushing into the house, crying. Turning to her, I said, "What's wrong?"

Almost bloody-red in the eyes, Janet said, "They are going to put me in jail."

Sensing something urgent and big, I focused on my female Black engineer wife with serious scrutiny. She then blurted out, crying, "I owe thousands of dollars in back payroll taxes to the IRS, and they came to my office." Janet had just revealed her lack of business acumen, and I was faced with a major problem that could derail the Daniels family's ascension.

I intentionally never did any business for Janet and her firm because I did not want to be blamed for its failure. Now, I was being dragged into her business, unwillingly to save her from jail and the IRS. Janet and I knew the IRS threat of jail time was real. Payroll tax violations are a serious sign of faulty business practices and put the entire public benefits system at risk if major violations occur. The IRS power to jail curtails this systematic threat, and Janet was now the target.

Ironically, after the first day, Janet never spoke of the payroll tax violations again. I assume business picked up, and she got a major receivable to cover the debt. Little did I know, she was sizing me up as a divorce target to cover her IRS debt.

During our initial divorce proceedings, Janet lied about several issues that still sickens me to my stomach. Janet lied in court papers that I hit her and bullied her. The grotesqueness of her outright lie bothered me because I was never an abusive husband. Janet and her attorney also told the judge that I was ill and my medical records were read into the court. I remind you, none of this was necessary as our divorce proceedings were uncontested. Usually, in an uncontested divorce, the judge checks to see if kids are involved. If kids are not involved, the consensual divorce boils down to splitting the assets and liabilities in half. As Janet's attorney continued maligning me in court, my mind drifted off to my garden. I detached myself from the lies in court by thinking of, of all things, my garden. I had planted a shade garden trail and had several types of perennial beds, and my garden was always my safe and peaceful place where I would relax. I was walking freely through my garden unharmed and proud of my work. Even Janet's master gardener parents were impressed with my garden. In my garden, I was also safe. As I mentally drifted back into the courtroom, I heard the judge say, "Why are we talking about Mr. Daniels's medical state of mind?"

The attorney said, "Your honor, Mrs. Daniels had to care for the livelihood of Mr. Daniels and should be compensated for the delivery of such services."

I could not believe my ears as Janet sat meekly like an innocent schoolgirl. Thankfully, the judge said, "This is nonsense. Motion denied. Let's move on to asset disposition."

The judge kept to the law and denied Janet's special exception and divided our assets.

Although Janet didn't get a special exception, she received a significant amount of money and could now pay her payroll taxes. She left the courtroom at a quick pace without a look my way. I thought I would never see her again, but I was wrong.

Even though I suspected that Janet was having an affair during the marriage, I could never prove it. In hindsight, I didn't care. I was Dr. Ken

Daniels, the established professor, and wired board member. People knew me, and I mattered to the community. She was a thief in the night, and I was not a fly by night player. I was anchored in the community and trying to bring resources to the Black community to make a difference. I was focused more on the superficial aspects of being married to a successful professional that I did not realize the family structure that was so important to me was slowly crumbling. I didn't want to accept the inevitable, but it was only a matter of time before I was forced to. As time passed, the signs of the inevitable became more concrete as Janet, and I grew further apart.

4

EVIL SPIRITS CIRCLE

I NEVER REALLY CONSIDERED myself to be a religious man, but I do believe in God. I know there is good and evil. I also knew that there is a physical world and a spirit world. At the point where I was physically unable to care for myself, these two worlds collided. Also, the spirit world knew of my vulnerability, and the spirits of this world or another world looked to take advantage of my weakness. Now let me be clear; I am the last person to believe in ghosts, paranormal activity, or non-science-based phenomenon. However, my time spent in the house alone on the 10 acres in remote Ashland, Virginia, changed my mind. I have no evidence, but I know that I was not alone in the house.

It all started as the grass around the house started to become overgrown. I was an avid gardener and kept the yard in pristine condition. On days when I forced myself, with what little energy I had left, I would walk to my bedroom window. It pained me to see my pristine garden covered with a lot of untidy plants and weeds. My soul was in those gardens. As the yard became overgrown, animals started to move closer and closer to the house. That is when the owl started making regular visits to the house every evening. It started as almost an evening melody every evening. In the beginning, it was soothing to know I was not alone. *Hoot, Hoot! Hoot! Hoot.* The owl would announce every evening. Sometimes when I would cut the grass at the house when healthy, I would see an owl. There were two owls: a huge white owl and a smaller brown owl. I never saw the evening owl, but I suspect it was one of these two. As time went on, the owl melodies became longer and louder, almost as if the owl was claiming the house and calling for me to leave.

Many nights were mysterious with strange noises outside, downstairs, and even in my room. My faith and a strong belief in my God and my elders gave me a hopefulness that I was protected. I knew I had angels protecting me during my time of weakness. I cannot prove it, but I knew I was never alone. Was I scared in the house by myself? Absolutely! There were several times that I was fearful for my life, given the forces that surrounded me. I remember one night when I heard a *bam* on my bedroom window on the second floor. *Bam! Bam!* It was a bunch of black crows flying into the window trying to break into the house. If the black crows had broken the window, I truly believe my life would have been in danger. This happened twice, and it gave me a resolve to get up out of bed and protect myself.

I lost a lot of weight during my illness. My normal weight was around 225 lbs., and my weight fell to around 199 lbs. I rarely went outside between May 2016 and October 2016. The mail collected in the mailbox and the grass grew taller and taller. A lot of things went wrong in 2016 for me. It was like a perfect storm of bad events. My dog, Bruno, died in January of 2016. My wife left me in May 2016, and we were divorced by November of 2016. I retired from my job of 30 years in May 2016, and the tractor I used to cut the grass stopped working. I know it sounds trivial about the tractor not working. However, I truly believed if I had gotten that tractor to work, I would have gotten out of the house more and worked on my gardens. As you might imagine, it just seemed like my whole world was crumbling. In retrospect, I was quite lucky as I was receiving a regular paycheck from the university, and I had plenty of soup and potato chips in the house. After the tractor broke, I just could not see buying a new tractor if I was not going to stay in the house. So, the grass just continued to grow and grow, and I worried about what the neighbors would think. The good news is that I had decided to fight my way back to life, even though my physical surroundings were deteriorating.

Around September 2016, I started to do some pushups, and my energy started to increase. My body still was not back to normal, but I started to feel like myself again. It took about a year for my body to recover from the low levels of testosterone. My doctor never knew why my body failed, and he never tried to give me a rationale.

Looking back, I probably should have sought different medical care as I did not get proper medical attention. Not only did I not get proper medical attention, it was commonly known that the entire Black community of Richmond did not get proper medical attention. Sometimes I would go to my Black primary care physician and wait an hour or more just for a routine medical check. Many Black elderly people would wait patiently in line to get medical care as they had no other options for quality medical care and the bus line in Richmond, Virginia did not travel into the richer county, Henrico, where the quality medical care had relocated. Many times my Black physician would say just call ahead and I will get you in the front of the line. I was appalled at such a suggestion and would never jump in front of the elderly people to get quicker care. I tell this story to illuminate the sad conditions that exist in the Black community for many people and it is tolerated by many Black professionals that should be ashamed of their standard of care for Black people.

Forgive me for going on a tangent but it is non inconsequential that I did not seek better medical care because it was just too hard to find in the Black medical community and the rural area where I was living. But the body is a wonderful machine, and if you give it time and the proper conditions, the body will correct itself. I thank God that I was relatively young with good health such that my body corrected itself and gave me a second chance at life. My second chance at life was not an accident and I truly believe everything happens for a reason to prepare me for a purpose driven life and the true meaning of why I was put on this earth. I don't mean to assert or imply that my life would be easier. In fact it would by its very nature be more challenging and require that I dig deep to use all of my talent and ability. However, the satisfaction and reward of being a God driven man and a purpose filled man outweighed any cost.

5

A SECOND CHANCE AT LIFE AND LOVE

WHY DID I DESERVE A SECOND chance at life or love? As I laid in bed, I really wanted to get up but I couldn't. I thought to myself I would never love again and what a horrible thought. I had so much love to give and I couldn't or I wouldn't get the chance. Because my body wasn't responding physically, in my mind, I thought I would never love a woman again, or more specifically, I thought I would never have sex again. As I think now, it was very shallow of me to equate sex with love but that was my thought process at the time. As I think back over my life, I guess I had a few instances of love. In reality, I don't think I ever really knew what love was. My family was a disjointed band of folks, and I never saw love openly expressed among my family members. Although I felt love from my mother, she did not overtly hug me or tell me that she loved me. Even my ex-wife didn't overtly show me love and was a cold fish most of the time, and her family was not a family that visibly demonstrated love physically with hugs or physical touching.

I think this lack of visible understanding of love played a major role in some of my decision making about my life partners that I sought after my divorce. However, I had a brand new opportunity in front of me to discover life along with love and I didn't want to waste it.

All my life, I wanted to make an impact in the minority communities of New Jersey and become a role model for positive economic development for the nation. So many times, I would ride around Newark, New Jersey, and see its potential to be a significant economic player in the competitive tri-state area. The area had a quality educational infrastructure of public and private high schools along with some top notch colleges such as Seton Hall Law School, New Jersey Institute of Technology (NJIT), and Rutgers, The State University of New Jersey: Newark Campus. However, there was a clear disconnect between the economic opportunity of the minority communities and the economic and educational infrastructure that surrounded towns like East Orange, Orange, and parts of Newark. Why was the disinvestment and blight that plagued these towns allowed to happen? For example, Orange had a vibrant hospital go bankrupt and completely vanish and leave behind acres of abandoned buildings along with a huge medical service gap in quality healthcare to the minority communities of Essex County. How could responsible leadership and government allow such significant institutions to fail so visibly and not respond with adequate solutions or policies to correct such devastating circumstances? These events of disinvestment and economic dislocation bothered me deeply. They bothered me so deeply, I was willing to risk my career, my life savings, and my professional reputation.

In my second chance at life, I wanted to be the economic savior of economic recovery in the forgotten and the damaged minority communities of New Jersey. I walked with the people of these communities, and I talked with the minorities of these communities. I was one of them. Even though I had a PhD, I was no better and the economic establishment treated me much the same way that they treated the common Black man in urban America as an Invisible man. These cold facts churned at my heart, and I decided to make an attempt at an institutional attempt at change by creating the Daniels Foundation for Impact Investments and Development. The Foundation is a 501c3 nonprofit attempting to provide affordable housing, educational programs such as financial literacy along with convenient sports activities for urban youth. Information on the Foundation can be found by searching for *www.daniels-foundation.org*. Hopefully, 2021 will be the year the Foundation gets traction and provides some real solutions to the economic chaos that plagues Black America and many other minority communities.

My second chance at life and love centered on two unknowns in my life. The first being my journey to find true love, and the second being my passion to be a true economic savior to the Black community. Although *Black Lives Matter* brought considerable attention to police brutality, it did not offer any credible policy recommendations for positive economic change. I wanted to be the voice of reason in the debate about how to move Black America and more importantly Black people forward to economic prosperity in America. In order to understand my passion for such a mission, it requires you go on the rise and fall of a modern Black man. As we go on this mission of finding a rational plan of economic development for Black America, it is important to have an understanding of some of the experiences Black men and Black people have had in America over the past 40 years. To go forward with a rational economic development plan, we must look back to have a sense of how and why we must move forward. In this sense, I offer my personal experiences and life as a vehicle to look at America and ourselves critically through some interesting stories. Please keep an open mind about the stories you are about to read as they are told in a manner meant to stimulate discussion about important topics and issues which confront Black America and Black men.

6

THE RISE

AT A VERY YOUNG AGE, I was a vibrant, confident, bold young man. I looked at the world as my oyster, and I attacked all my activities with vigor and hunger. I loved school and my classmates. I could not get enough knowledge or the attention that came from success.

In my early years, I was cultivated by motivated teachers who just happened to be White. I adored one of my elementary school teachers at Washington School, Ms. Jewel. She would bring us matzo crackers with butter, and I would work hard to be first in line for our reward. At an early age, I learned that rewards were coupled with success, and I was determined to outwork anyone to get the prizes in life.

This work ethic extended from school to the playing field and the games that kids play in elementary school. I was competitive at kickball, volleyball, dodgeball, baseball, football, and basketball. Basketball came easy to me, and I learned to play with the older boys early in life at Washington Playground in East Orange, New Jersey. Back in the 1960s, Washington Playground was an oasis of activity for Black children. Kids could play sports, games such as chess and checkers, or just swing on the swings and talk. I was at peace at Washington Playground, and I flourished there in the safety it provided me. It is important to note that my school and place of play was a safe environment for me. This comfort level allowed me to be an innocent young man without any distractions from the street, such as drugs, sex, or criminality.

I grew up in the 1960s when drugs, sex, and crime derailed many Black men's lives, leaving them without the skills to move up the economic ladder. I was determined not to follow that path. My father also made sure of that. He was an educator, a champion for education, and became one of the first Black school principals in New Brunswick, New Jersey. From him, I developed an aptitude for math and hard work. These skills would come in handy while studying for my Ph.D. in Economics from the University of Connecticut. My drive to better myself also stemmed from a stark realization that I was relatively poor economically to my classmates at Fairfield University and the University of Connecticut. I vividly remember putting cardboard in my sneakers while in high school to plug the holes so the snow would not get to my toes. I also remember my mother mending my brothers hand-me-down sweater so that they would fit me neatly. It impacted me so much psychologically so that at the age of 45, I still had my white prom suit from high school along with several sweaters that I wore in high school. I had trained myself never to let go of any clothing because they might be needed for a rainy day. My sense of my humble beginnings never left me even as I transcended into a higher economic class. I never forgot where I came from and the sacrifices my family made to get me there.

Although I was recognized as one of the better students in the school, it was my work ethic that allowed me to prosper. By the time I got to middle school, I was a polished student. I was trained in music, as my father insisted that I play an instrument. I played the trombone and earned the first seat. Mr. Preston Williams was the music teacher and noticed that I had a gift for music and tried to get me to commit more time and effort to the trombone. However, all the boys played basketball after school, and basketball was my first love. Over time, the trombone fell by the wayside, and basketball became my primary activity along with baseball.

I wanted to play football, but my mother would not have her son getting hit in the head. In retrospect, Mom knew best because football is a dangerous activity for young men. Basketball took a higher priority in my life when I made the travel basketball team in East Orange, the East Orange Little Lads. Travel basketball was the top competition in the state, and sometimes the competition got to be on a national level. We frequently traveled to New York to play the best teams in Harlem or the Bronx. It was during this time that I started to develop into a good basketball player.

After middle school, I made the freshman and junior varsity basketball teams. I worked extremely hard on my basketball game every day. I even heard the neighbor saying one day, "Here goes that Daniels boy dribbling that ball up the hill again."

My hard work paid off, and I was the MVP of the first state junior varsity basketball tournament in New Jersey. We beat Neptune in the championship game, and my above-average play was starting to grab the attention of some small colleges but, more importantly, Coach Lester.

Coach Lester was the varsity basketball coach, and he was well respected in the town and all over the state. He was an icon, and he determined who made the varsity basketball team. After the junior varsity game, Coach Lester smiled at me and said, "Good game." I smiled back, but I was bursting with pride inside. Coach Lester knew I could play competitive basketball.

I continued to excel in my school studies, and I earned a top 10 ranking in high school academically. I was placed in all the honors classes, and the work was rigorous. One year, I had a class load of physics, advanced calculus, and advanced history. Although I attended an urban high school, there were pockets of excellence for some of the students. My cohort of classmates and classes were very different from the rest of high school. Most of my friends cut classes and rarely attended school regularly. By the end of my sophomore year, I was a fine-tuned athlete and a high achieving scholar in high school.

Entering my junior year, I had so much anticipation for the basketball program. East Orange High School was ranked number 1 in the nation by *Street & Smith's Basketball Magazine* primarily due to our talented seniors. Coach Lester recognized the talent in the high school and announced to all tryout attendees that he was only taking ten basketball players for the 1977 East Orange High School basketball team. I must laugh at this memory because, on the day of the tryout, about 100 guys tried out for the basketball team. So, 90 good basketball players did not make the varsity team. But I remember the fierceness of that tryout like it was yesterday, and I was determined to make the varsity basketball team.

Guys were kicking and clawing for every advantage trying to stand out to Coach Lester. I still remember Coach Lester posting the team names on the hallway board and the reaction of several guys. Some guys cried upon not seeing their name on the list. As I walked up to the list, I saw my name about midway down. It read Ken Daniels, 6'2", guard. I was so excited as I had achieved a dream and goal.

I was a Panther, or more accurately, I was an EO Panther. This meant something in a small competitive town, and it paved the way for my college basketball scholarship to Fairfield University. All the years of nurturing the hard work ethic, the rigorous academics, and the cultural awareness of being a prideful Black man produced a young gifted, and Black talent. I truly felt like I was somebody with a future, and the future was bright. I was on the rise.

My junior year of high school was filled with promise. I continued to excel academically, and my basketball career rose with the team. The 1977 East Orange basketball team was one of the best teams in New Jersey, and college scouts started recruiting me during my senior year.

Three universities emerged as really interested in me, and I was a confused young man. Lehigh University, Iona University, and Fairfield University offered me full 4-year basketball scholarships during my senior year. I was proud to help my family out financially, and the scholarship was real money. Ironically, I do not remember my parents being involved in my recruiting process as I handled most of the correspondence.

I do remember one conversation with my mother about William and Mary University. The coach from William and Mary, Bruce Parkhill, called and asked to speak with my mom. The conversation was very short. After hanging up the phone, my mom said, "You will never go back down South for school."

My mom grew up in Luray, Virginia, and she told me stories of the racism that she and her family experienced in the Commonwealth of Virginia. The racism was so bad that my mom's family sent her to a boarding school in Bordentown, New Jersey, to get a decent education.

Education was always a common denominator for the Daniels family, and my mom was the valedictorian of her graduating class. I looked up to my mom because she is book smart, beautiful, and street smart. I took most of her savviness and kept my eye on the prize. I yearned to get out of the urban ghetto and raise my family with opportunities that I never had. Later in life, I would accomplish this goal by sending both of my kids to private school, giving them a quality education.

I graduated in 1978 from East Orange High School, a high school with meager resources but a big heart. It gave me a solid foundation to succeed in the competitive educational environment of higher education. High school also gave me all the other perks of being a well-known person. I dated several girls but never really had a steady girlfriend. I went to the prom with Giselle, and we had a good time but never really connected. I went off to Fairfield University without any solid connection to my hometown except for the relationship with my mother and father. I had several good friends in Joe Jordan and Chris Orrell, but we drifted away in our separate directions and interests. I was on my way to becoming a solid young adult, and I was ready to reap the rewards of my investments.

7

MY FIRST LOVES

MOST MEN HAVE A FIRST LOVE. Not me. I had two. Both were special, and I have fond memories of each of them. The first was Deidre, and she was a pretty, voluptuous country girl who was also a tomboy. Deidre played basketball on the girls' basketball team. Often the boys' basketball team would practice right after the girls' basketball team, so we saw each other often, and we would joke or play around with each other. I did not pursue Deidre as a girlfriend, and we never really dated as boyfriend and girlfriend. But I loved some Deidre because she was cute, innocent, and funny. She lived on the other side of town, which was called "Down the Way," in the projects, and it was a long way from my house, which was close to Orange, New Jersey, and Orange Park. Deidre lived almost in Newark, New Jersey, and the neighborhood could be kind of rough if you got caught there at the wrong time of day or night. Deidre's perseverance to remain innocent despite the unfortunate circumstance of her neighborhood was an attraction to me. She was close friends with my friend Billy Marshall who also lived "Down the Way". Billy was a very mature guy for our age, and he was always trying to hook-up Deidre and I. Billy also played on the basketball team with me, and he would always kid me that Deidre was asking about me. I did not pay much attention to Billy, as during my senior year, I was focused on school and basketball.

Then there was Kathy. She was a junior, and I had a crush on her. Love can be complicated and confusing sometimes. Kathy was a beautiful, sassy young woman with a spirit-filled with fun, fun, and fun. Kathy also lived "Down the Way," and her mother was an alcoholic with an abusive boyfriend. I always felt sorry for Kathy as I always felt she was under siege at her house with problems. Her mother was one of the sweetest people I ever met in the world, and I could tell she loved Kathy. It was clear Kathy got her sassiness from her mom and her environment. Although Kathy came from a difficult environment, I knew she would be successful because her personality was infectious. If you talked to Kathy for five minutes, you could not take your eyes off her because she was an alpha personality. Deidre, on the other hand, was a shy and meek young lady who sounded country and out of place in the urban landscape.

I think it is fair to say that I loved Deidre and Kathy as a young man but never made a long-lasting connection with any of them because I was a young man on a mission. A mission to achieve some level of success outside the norm of just being a basketball player. I think this is what drove my dedication to my schoolwork besides basketball. I had a love for learning. This complicated my relationship with Kathy as I never really had the time to be with her, and Kathy was a busy mind with places to go. Our relationship did not have a chance at surviving.

Billy Marshall was a persistent guy, and he was a facilitator. Billy was always doing some transaction, and you never really knew what he was up to. He was a really good guy, and I trusted him like a brother. One day Billy came to me, and he said, "I was talking to Deidre, and she wants you."

It was not every day that a young woman offered her body for love to a young man. I was quite stunned by Billy as he uttered the words in such a cavalier manner. I was wracking my brain, wondering how this would be possible since most teenagers have no place to make love, so they hook up in cars on lonely streets or use a friend's house if the parents are not home. I remember smiling at Billy and saying, "That's nice. Deidre is a sweet girl. I like her."

He went on to describe how she liked me, and he wanted us to hook up at his house because his mom worked a lot. Now at this point, I was not sure whether Billy was trying to facilitate a hookup just for fun or whether Deidre was seeking me out.

The next day before practice, I saw Deidre, and we began to talk. Every time Deidre spoke, her country drawl made me weak in the knees because she was just such an innocent thing. Then Deidre said something that almost made me fall. She asked me, "Did you talk to Billy?"

I smiled and said, "Yeah, we chatted a bit. Why?"

I will never forget her face or her expression on her sweet face as she said, "I want you to be the man that takes my virginity."

Just to be sure, I said, "What?"

Deidre, looking at me firmly and smiling, said, "You heard me. I want you to be the man that takes my virginity."

After looking stunned for a couple of seconds, I mumbled out, "OK."

Deidre was determined to lose her virginity quickly. She smiled and said, "Good," in a sweet country, drawl. I was smiling from ear to ear. She continued, "Just talk to Billy, and he'll let you know where to go."

Billy and Deidre were good friends. You could almost say that Billy was her brother. Billy and Deidre had a conversation about her losing her virginity, and I just happened to be the guy. Hallelujah! Right after practice, Billy, the facilitator, pulled me aside, whispering, "Look, I got it all set up. Just meet me at my house after school on Tuesday." He looked me in the eye, and without mentioning a word, I gave him a "pound," which was an urban handshake for OK.

Billy and I had talked on Friday, and before you knew it, Tuesday had arrived. I was nervous the entire weekend and could not even look my mother in the face. If my mom knew her baby boy was having sex, she would go ballistic. I kept my cool and did my chores. We practiced on Saturday as usual, and Billy just kept grinning at me knowing our secret.

Tuesday morning, I dressed extra carefully and paid attention to my hygiene. I came from a family of four boys, and money was tight. I did not have an elaborate clothes collection. I had a selection of sweaters along with hand-me-down pants and shirts. Most of my clothes came from my older brothers, who were twins. My father was an elementary school principal and was the first Black principal in New Brunswick, New Jersey, and a pioneer. However, we lived on a meager principal salary for a family of six. As I headed out of the house, my mom said, "You look nice today."

Startled, I said, "Thanks, mom," and ran out of the house.

I think a Mom always knows when something is up. I quickly got into my fast walk. I lived about 7 miles from the high school, which was a brisk 40-minute walk. East Orange had no busing service in the 1970s, and most students walked to school. I had a set route every day and picked up my buddy Joe Jordan every day at about 10 minutes into my walk. Joe knew the rules, and he was always ready to fast walk. Meeting Joe without stopping or breaking a stride, we walked to school every day during rain, sleet, or shine. During our walk, I mentioned Deidre to Joe, and he said, "She's kind of fat."

Deidre was heavily built and very sexy with the plumpest cheeks. I adored her, and Joe's words cut me the wrong way. I ignored Joe, and we kept walking and talking along the way. As usual, we arrived at the high school on time for class.

Classes went quickly that day, and we did not have a practice that Tuesday for some reason. Billy Marshall was waiting for me after my last class and walked with me to my locker. Looking at me seriously, he said, "You ready?"

Being as brash as I could be, I replied, "I'm always ready."

Billy and I walked quickly to his house and said little along the way. After about 20 minutes, we opened his front door, and Deidre was inside waiting. Billy never went into the house. Quickly, Billy gave me a hug, a pound, and was gone.

Deidre was sitting on the couch, and the house was dimly lit. She said, "Don't you look cute."

I laughed and hugged her. Sitting on the couch, we chatted a bit. Deidre asked me, "Do you want something to drink?"

I responded, "Sure."

I was not nervous, but I was not sexually active. Deidre brought me a

Coke, and we began to kiss and hug on the couch. We made out for a minute, and then she looked at me, saying, "Are you nervous?"

I said, "Why would I be nervous?"

For some reason, I was at peace with Deidre. She looked beautiful. She had on a revealing peach-colored blouse and shorts, which revealed her sexy legs. Deidre was a straight-up tomboy, but she was also very feminine, and I was turned on by her look and voice. Looking Deidre in the eyes, I told her not to be nervous. Then I kissed her on the cheek and grabbed her hand. Slowly we walked to the bedroom, and I sat her on the bed. I turned on the radio and the perfect song was playing. I remember the song like it was yesterday; *Love Won't Let Me Wait* by Major Harris. Slowly, we laid down together and kissed and hugged. I felt her love for me, and she seemed attracted to me. I unbuttoned her blouse, and Deidre's massive breast fell in my face. To be quite honest, I did not know what to do with such massive tits. I was not an experienced lover at age 17. I did not turn 18 until July 24th of 1978, and Deidre lost her virginity around October 1977. We kissed for a while, and I finally got undressed, and we made love. I know we made love for a few songs. I can remember caressing Deidre to the Major Harris song, and I remember her eyes as I penetrated her and heard a slight moan. I tried to be gentle as it was her first time. I held Diedre tight while we made love, and eventually, we fell asleep together.

Years later, when I was fifty, I saw Deidre, and she smiled. She said, "I am glad you were the man that took my virginity."

I laughed and asked, "Was I any good?"

She replied, "You were the best and gentle."

I felt relieved as I always liked Deidre and our relationship. We hugged and exchanged numbers. Deidre was married with kids now. Life had been hard on her. She was no longer innocent and had just recently recovered from drug addiction to crack cocaine. I felt relieved that I had, for the most part, lived an uneventful life up to that point. Little did I know that in about another ten years, I would also have my downfall and life challenges.

As I think back on that special moment in Billy Marshall's house with Deidre, it was probably one of the few honest, pure acts of love in my life. Lying on the bed with Deidre, I was at peace, and I felt true love. As we got dressed, we did not say much to each other. We both had to get home quickly to avoid the wrath of our mothers. I gave her a strong hug and kissed her lips firmly. Waving bye, I slipped out of the bedroom and out the front door.

I started my brisk walk down Munn Avenue, and quickly I was by the basketball court by Elmwood Park. Several guys I knew were playing basketball, and I wanted to stop and play. My mind quickly reverted to my first love and my challenges ahead. I was feeling pretty good as I walked from "Down the Way" to "Up the Way." The "Up the Way" part of East Orange was a pristine Black middle-class neighborhood in the 1970s. The streets were tree-lined, and single-family homes lined both sides of the street. Little did I know that my life would be impacted by this dichotomy in the Black American experiences of the 1970s.

America was a country in transition, and my experiences would be strongly coupled with this American destiny. Finally, making it home, my mom greeted me at the door. She hit me with her usual statement, "Kenneth Nolan Daniels, where have you been?"

I rarely lied to my mother. I replied, "Oh, I have just been playing with some friends," and I ran up the steps to my room. Falling on my bed exhausted, I thought of my day and my first love. Still mesmerized by my first pure love, I fell asleep.

Then there was Kathy. I had a crush on the charismatic Kathy Friedman. All the guys did. Kathy was a year younger than me, and she had an eclectic group of friends since she was so magnetic. She attracted the good, the bad, and the ugly. Her family's economic status brought her into contact with all kinds of characters, and I had a strong feeling that her mother's boyfriend, Will, was a pimp.

I enjoyed my talks with Kathy as her desire to persevere was clear. We shared the same values in excelling at school. She was also protective of her destiny and her family members. Although they lived in multi-family housing, the Friedmans were a tight-knit, loving family. Kathy hung with Toi, who dated one of my best friends, Nate Brown. Nate was a handsome chocolate skin athletic brother. Unfortunately, he was not a good student in school and fell by the wayside as we progressed through high school.

Kathy, Toi, Nate, and I would often meet at Nate's house and hang out.

Nate came from a single-parent home, and his mother was never home. Unfortunately for me, my mother did not work and was always home. This led to Kathy, and I was always hanging in the park or at Nate's house. I was smitten with Kathy Friedman from the day I met her. We met after a basketball game, and she quickly targeted me with some sharp wit and tongue that spun my head. Kathy was a sweet soul, but you could tell she had experienced pain.

When I kissed Kathy, I could see the pain in her eyes. I am sure there is a story of her pain, but we never discussed it. I courted Kathy hard, but I had competition for her affection from a guy named Adolph. Adolph was a good-looking streetwise character from "Down the Way." In some ways, he and Kathy's personality fit like a glove. Both were charismatic and charming in an extroverted way. I, on the other hand, was more of an introvert but could be outgoing when provoked. And boy, did Kathy provoke me in so many ways. I did not know it at the time, but sometimes love can be competitive, and I had to fight to win Kathy's attention. In some ways, I think Kathy was just with me because I was a popular basketball player. This thought always was stuck in the back of my head. Kathy was briefly a cheerleader during part of my basketball career, so sometimes we would pass each other near the gym. Kathy was almost the opposite of Deidre in every aspect. She was skinny and barely had a chest. But whenever she opened her mouth, she had the gift of gab and was probably the most fun person to be around. Kathy and I dated briefly, and I like to think I won the love triangle for a short period. In the long run, I must give the battle to Mr. Adolph as I think he won her heart.

Although I was not the love of Kathy's life, we were attracted to each other and made love often. I should probably correct it and say we had sex often. Kathy was skinny and limber, which made her an excellent sex partner. She also acted experienced and taught me a thing or two. I could not get enough of Kathy Friedman. While Deidre and I only made love once, it was almost perfect. Kathy and I made love frequently, and it was imperfect. I do not know why I never got together with Deidre again, probably because I was infatuated with Kathy. Eventually, I lost the interest of Kathy, and our attraction waned.

Eventually, my sexual interaction with Kathy became very transactional and more for my pleasure than love. Looking back, I wonder why I made the choices I made and what they reflected on my preferences. I would classify Kathy as the closest relationship I got with a young woman in high school, and I am not sure she was my girl. I bounced around to a few other girls after that, but there was no love connection. I went to the prom with Giselle because she asked me, and I said yes. However, Giselle and I were never steady and hardly knew each other. Shortly after high school, she got pregnant by a close friend and got married at an early age. When I heard this, I felt I dodged a bullet. I clearly could not have children at an early age and fulfill my dreams. So, coming out of high school, I was truly an open book on love. Although I had experiences, I had no clarity on what love was or what it took to maintain love. Many who know me may find this ironic because they thought that I was a "Playboy" and had many girlfriends. Quite the contrary, I had my sight on getting out of East Orange with no strings to hold me back.

THE FORMATIVE YEARS

MY FATHER AND MOTHER WERE the best parents a son could ask for. They were both fiercely protective of their sons, and I shudder to think what would have happened to our family if I had told them of my secret. I think it is important to talk about my mom, my dad, and their union as it had such an important impact on my development and life. My mom was born a mountain girl in the Blue Ridge Mountains of Virginia in the 1930s. This area is royally known as Shenandoah, reminiscent of John Boy and the Waltons on the television show, and the mountains are majestic. My mom used to tell me stories of her father, John Taylor, and the harsh mountain life they endured. In early Luray for Black people, you were either from the Taylor clan or the Porter clan. My mother was one of five girls of the Taylor clan, and the Taylor clan saw the potential of Gwendolyn, my mother, at a young age. The family sent her off to Bordentown Finishing School, in Bordentown, New Jersey, where she matriculated as the valedictorian and met my father. My mother was super smart and sharp as a tack. She gave up a career at Westinghouse to raise four Black men. My mom's mannerisms were cool, calm, and collective as she never got flustered by any hardship.

She would tell me stories about how cold it got on the mountain and that if her father could not make a fire to heat the home, they could die from the cold. Although my mother came from Luray, I saw pictures of her sisters in elegant dresses and fine clothes. I asked my mother where the nice clothes came from, and she said, "Mama Dear made them."

Mama Dear was the matriarch of the Taylor clan, my grandmother, and she lived with us in New Jersey before she died of cancer. I remember her vividly as a strong cerebral woman who had a lot of energy for an elderly woman who was sick. She was funny but direct and sent me to the corner store, Carmen's, to buy her cigarettes occasionally.

One day Mama Dear gave me money to get her cigarettes at the corner store. I think I was about seven at the time, and I lost the money on the way to the store. Little did I know, but I was about to get a Luray lesson in responsibility. Approaching her in the bed, I said, "Mama, Dear, I lost the money."

She said, "Pick your head up, boy. This is what I want you to do." She continued, "Now, are you listening?"

I sheepishly nodded my head. Mama Dear then grabbed me firmly by the face, not in a painful way but a direct way. She said, "I want you to tell Carmen exactly what happened and don't you get it wrong. Tell him you lost the money and that Mama Dear wants her cigarettes."

She softly let go of my face and said, "Hurry on now."

I had my instructions, and at the age of seven, I knew I had to come back with some cigarettes, or I would be in trouble. Carmen's was the Italian parlor store on Sanford Street in East Orange. Most Italians had left East Orange and fled into the hills of Livingston or West Orange as my father described it. As you entered Carmen's store, a bell warmly jingled, and the counter seats were set up for root beer floats, Italian hot dogs, and many other deli delights. At the cash register was a bounty of penny candy, and behind the register were many cigarettes like Marlboro, Camels, and Lucky Stripe.

Carmen knew my family well and respected all in the neighborhood. Looking up to Carmen, I said, "Mama Dear told me to tell you that she needs her cigarettes, but I lost the money."

Carmen said, "Is that so? Is that what she said?"

I countered back, forcefully, "Yeah. That is what she told me."

Without hesitation, Carmen reached for two packs of cigarettes and placed them in my hand. He said, "Tell Mama Dear, I said hello, and don't drop the cigarettes."

Smiling at Carmen, I turned quickly and ran down Edgar Street with a pack of cigarettes in each hand. As I entered the house, I was out of breath but plopped the cigarettes on Mama Dear's lap and fell on the floor tired. She peered over the bed and looked down at me with a big smile. With glowing eyes, she said, "Now that's how you listen. Always listen, and you can never go wrong." Lying on my back on the floor, I looked up at Mama Dear with a contented smile. I did not understand all that she said, but I understood that given instruction, you better get it right. My mom entered the room and said, "Kenneth, get up off that floor and leave Mama Dear alone."

Mama Dear hid her cigarettes and gave me a wink and a smile. I scattered out of the room to the back porch. Later that year, Mama Dear died, and we buried her in Luray, Virginia, on the Taylor family plot in the Negro cemetery. I never forgot the trip and always remembered the winding road and the majestic mountains. My lasting memory of the trip was the cows by the house chewing on some straw. I remember me trying to touch the cow's mouth when my mother walked up and firmly directly grabbed my face. Turning me gently with my face in her hand, she said, "Now, are you listening?"

Inwardly, I thought Mama Dear had not left us at all; she was still grabbing my face.

My father was a self-made man, but he was groomed by my grandmother, Priscilla Cooper, to be an articulate and successful professional Black man. Although my grandmother made her fortune in the beauty supply business, she was determined that her two sons, Henry and Arthur, would ascend professionally above the field of trade. As a young boy, I never knew why my grandmother did not have the same last name as my father. Later, I would learn that she remarried after my grandfather's death. Priscilla Cooper grew up in the segregated America of Black and

White and prospered in the Black beauty industry. However, she wanted more but was restricted by the cultural norms of Whites refusing to do business with Black people, let alone a Black woman. These restrictions never caused my grandmother, Priscilla Cooper, to question or ponder her destiny. Ascending from a strong economic foundation, Priscilla Copper would prosper and be called the "Maggie Walker" of Philadelphia.

Maggie Walker was one of the first Black millionaires developing the lucrative Black hair products industry. My father was brought up on the tough Main Street of Camden, New Jersey, not far from Campbell's Soup. He told me stories of him gambling "craps" as a young man, and he teetered on the criminality line given its proximity to his family home. Priscilla Cooper would not let her two Black sons fall victim to the creeping criminal elements of Camden. Similarly, my mother, my father, and his brother were sent off to Bordentown Finishing School to escape the growing ghetto in Camden due to the restrictive anti-Negro policies at the Federal, State, and local levels. Given the good fortune of his mother, my father arrived at Bordentown Finishing School as a classically trained musician and student. He prospered in the productive all Black educational environment.

I clearly remember my father taking my brothers and me to stay at my grandmother's Camden house. It was a classic brick Philadelphia row house, but the interior was lavishly decorated with crystals and fine china. As you might imagine, my grandmother did not appreciate any rough house play that could jeopardize her sizable collection of fine items. I immediately got the message from my grandmother in a direct way to sit down and do not get antsy or else.

You might ask, or else what? Well, my brothers, Keith and Kevin, ignored the warning as you might imagine and got antsy for a pair of energetic teenagers. It did not take long before my brother Kevin pushed Keith, and boom, the elegant crystal shattered on the floor.

Without knowing it, my brothers had just ordered a Camden discipline lesson, and it was not going to be pretty. My grandmother worked at the hairdressing lounge and school next to the house. Although she did not need to, Priscilla Cooper trained a legion of hair care professionals in the Camden and Philadelphia area. The Daniels name was associated with training slaves in various trade fields in the Petersburg, Virginia, and Boydton, Virginia areas.

Upon arriving home from work, my grandmother immediately noticed the broken crystal. I was still sitting in the same elegant chair. She instructed me to sit before she left. So, she veered off me as a target and focused on my brothers. Walking up to my brothers, she asked, "What happened?"

My brothers, being mischievous, did not answer, and had the nerve to snicker a laugh. Little did they know, they made a mistake. Grabbing Kevin by his ear, my grandmother dragged him to the closet and made him grab a broom. All I could see was Kevin's ear getting redder and redder, and he was lifted off his feet. As she dragged Kevin back to the broken glass, she let go and snatched my brother Keith by his ear to the same closet for a dustpan. Keith was not as tough as Kevin, and he immediately began to cry. Kevin began sweeping as Priscilla Cooper dragged a crying Keith by his ear to the broken glass. My brothers quickly swept up the broken glass and sat quietly next to me, except for a whimpering Keith.

Silence consumed the house as my grandmother proceeded to cook dinner for my father and his sons. You could hear a pin drop. The house was so quiet, and my grandmother ignored us and didn't say a word as we sat in the chairs aligned in a row against the chair-railed wall.

My brothers' ears beamed red like the nose of Rudolph, the Red-Nosed Reindeer, and they were clearly in pain. The doorbell rang, and my grandmother said, "Y'all better not move."

I froze as she walked by and opened the door for my father. "Henry," she said while showering him with kisses, "Come on in. Dinner is ready for you."

My father walked in and put his hat upon the hat stand. Peering to the chair-railed wall where we were lined up like prisoners, my father did not say a word as if he was familiar with the punishment. My grandmother put the food on the table and said, "Boys, go wash your hands and sit at the table."

My father walked with us to the bathroom, where we all washed our hands and sat at the table with my grandmother at the head of the table. She said, "Henry, please say grace."

My father loved to say grace, and he went on for about five minutes, blessing the food. "Amen," said my grandmother, and he knew it was time to stop.

The food was delicious, and I ate all my food. Keith and Kevin did not feel like eating and smothered their emotions to not provoke my grandmother again. We had to get back to North Jersey, so Dad and I kissed his mother and got in the car. As we drove up the road, my father burst into a burst of big, loud laughter and said, "I guess you boys learned not to mess with my mother."

He then went on to elaborate on how strict his mother was as she kept them out of trouble in Camden. He then said, "I see she almost tore your ear off. I know how that feels, and it hurts."

Keith was still whimpering, and Kevin sat grumpily like he was mad. We all listened to my dad tell stories about his mother, growing up in Camden, and the discipline he endured as a child. It was clear that Priscilla Cooper was in charge anytime you were in her presence. The violence she delved out was not merciful and the message sent was 'control yourself or be controlled.' I did not have any deep emotions for my father's mother as I did Mama Dear. Even at a young age, I knew right from wrong.

The union of my father and mother seemed like a match made in heaven. Although my father came from an urban environment and my mom from a primarily rural environment, they had a lot in common. Both showed a high aptitude for learning, and both were ambitious in their way. My father wanted to break down color barriers and penetrate the professional ranks that had been sequestered away from Black people in a systematic way. My mom wanted to use her wisdom to build a traditional family to take advantage of the burgeoning opportunities slowly being made available to the Black middle class.

In their way, my mother and father were both pioneers as America transitioned away from the dichotomy of a White only or a Black only theatre of play. My mother and father had a fairy tale romance but had a modest wedding at my Aunt Hazel O'Brien's house in East Orange, New Jersey. They formed a perfect union as a couple and visibly showed affection towards each other. They were in love but were they ready for the task of raising four boys in a rapidly changing world. My father was the sole breadwinner and always busy. Did my father not provide proper attention to his sons due to work? This is a fair question to ask.

My father did his due diligence and found good housing with a good school in a primarily Black neighborhood. The "Up the Way" neighborhood was beautiful, and I had two older big brothers to guide me and protect me. My brothers were fraternal twins. They did everything together, good or bad. To this day, my brothers are inseparable and protect each other at all costs. I was in awe of my older brothers. Both of my brothers were big, and as a team, they commanded their space well. They were also smart guys in different ways. Kevin was really smart, and he assessed his situations quickly to act to his advantage. Keith was more cerebral than Kevin, and as a deep thinker, he did very well in school. These traits made my brothers competitive. I looked up to them, and they guided me as I played sports at Washington Playground around the corner. Although my brothers were tied at the hip, I was a close sidekick never far behind.

Kevin was the oldest twin by a few hours, and as the alpha twin, he led my other brother Keith most of the time. Kevin was a very smart guy but got into some trouble in his youth, and trouble followed him as a young adult until he entered the Navy. I will call Kevin the evil twin because he had a demonic type personality, and I will tell you why.

At an early age, Kevin got into mischief often and developed a penchant for pornography. What kind of kid gets involved with pornography around puberty? I don't know where he got the Playboy pictures, but he cut out a large number of Playboy pictures and taped them to the front door of Kenneth Hayes' house and a couple of nearby neighbors on Kenwood Street. This transgression happened before middle school, so Kevin was a troublemaker in his elementary school years, and his behavior had an impact on my brother, his twin, Keith.

Growing up, Keith was the nicer twin. He was personable and smart. Unfortunately, Keith was easily swayed by Kevin. My father set Keith up to be an engineer at the prestigious Steven's Technical Institute in Hoboken, New Jersey. Keith was excelling in college when an unfortunate event. At Steven's Tech, Keith's roommate was a business-savvy White boy trying to make a buck selling marijuana. As Kevin visited Keith in college, he learned of the lucrative marijuana business. After this visit a robbery occurred with Keith's roommate and the marijuana was stolen from Keith's roommate at gunpoint! The college did not waste time. Although they could not prove that Keith actively participated in the robbery, they expelled him from Steven's Tech.

My father was crushed. My father prided himself on the fact that he was a pioneer Black principal in New Jersey and a scholar graduate from West Virginia State University and Rutgers University. This was a blow to him. He had to face the harsh reality of the path his two eldest sons had chosen. Instead of wallowing in self-pity, he took action. To his credit, he knew instinctively that they both needed discipline and directed both of my brothers into the armed services and thus changed the course of their lives. After witnessing my father's disappointment with my brothers, I was determined to be a good student and a successful person.

As I grew up with my twin brothers, who were 13 years old at the time, they noticed the natural affinity and loved my dad had for me. My mom said I was almost an identical image of my dad, and she displayed pictures of my dad and I next to each other around the house. She was clearly trying to reinforce the resemblance. Although I cannot say my brothers disliked me because of this fatherly affection, they were aware of the attention I was getting.

I was only nine years old at the time, but I was advanced for my age. I was doing well in school, and I was built to run, jump, and fight. Although I wasn't the fastest, I had cat-like awareness and quickness, which made me a quick study. At nine years old, I made the Little League baseball team for the older boys and beat out the much older Paul Grandy, who would later become an outstanding doctor, for the right field position. Years later, in jest, Paul thanked me for taking his spot so he could study more. In hindsight, we all benefited from the social activities at Washington Park. I followed my brothers around like a happy puppy dog, and they protected me and shepherded me in the right direction. Suddenly, all this changed one day and changed me for the rest of my life.

I loved our house. It was a beautiful white colonial in a nice section of East Orange. Also, we each had our room, which was an improvement from our previous house at 37 Edgar Street. Dad took meticulous care of the house, and mom was the quintessential housewife. As kids, we would ride the dumb waiter up and down like an elevator. My friends started spreading rumors that we had an elevator in our house.

When we moved into this house, my mom had just had another baby; my younger brother Kyle was born. My parents had their hands full with four Black boys in the late 1960s. One year earlier, Martin Luther King had been shot, and the rioters burned Newark to the ground. I remember watching it on television. It was violent as the National Guard and police violated the rights of the protesters. Little did I know that I would also feel the pain of violation.

9

THE FIRST TEAR

I CONSIDERED OUR HOME at 100 Park End Place to be a warm and safe place. That is why it is hard for me, fifty years later, to describe the brutality I endured in our family home. I was just nine years old when it happened. I was raped and sodomized by not just one but two individuals in my family. It happened in my parents' bedroom when they were not at home. I had gone into their room to play when they entered and locked the door.

I cried. For the first time I can remember, I cried. I still cry today, but there are no tears, just an empty, raw wound that continues to fester. It is as if I can hear drums in the distance. The drums are faded, but as time passes, the sound gets louder and louder. Suppress it as I might, it jolted me awake in 2016 after I became ill after returning from a business trip to South Africa. As the doctors tried to figure out my illness, I was sent to a few specialists, and I would have to fill out the medical forms. The question on one of the medical forms triggered my visceral reaction, "Have you ever been sexually assaulted?"

I stared down on the form as if I was trying to read English for the first time. The pen fell from my finger, my chest tightened, and my breathing became labored. For a few minutes, it almost seemed as if I had blacked out. Here I was, a grown man with a hidden secret for over five decades. I wanted so badly to answer yes to the sexual assault question. But instead, I circled no.

I was only nine years old at the time, and I didn't understand what was happening. The rape didn't last long, but as long as I live, I will never forget it. They told me it was a secret game. They told me it would not hurt and that everyone played the game. I remember them getting the jar of Vaseline, and I remember the pain when they raped me one after the other. I remember screaming for them to "Stop." I screamed and screamed. I kept screaming, "No!" but they held me down. I tried to fight them off, but I was powerless. After the sexual assault, they urged me not to talk to mom or dad about our secret. I remember crying after they finished. I remember walking out of my parent's room down the hall to my bedroom and sobbing uncontrollably. I remember burying my face down in the pillow to muffle the noise so they would not hear how much pain I was in. Although I didn't know what had just happened, I remember for the first time, feeling fearful in my own home. The trust I had with my family members had been lost now.

I never spoke of this to my mom or dad. I felt like I had done something bad, almost like it was my fault. Today I know better. I realize now that suppressing childhood sexual assault is very damaging to the psyche of the adult who was raped as a child. It is essential to get therapy to deal with childhood traumas like this.

I did blame my family members for the rape and my loss of innocence. My childhood was no longer "normal." Our household was primarily used by my brothers and a few family members. Although I knew my family members had the potential to do bad things, I never expected they would plot and plan to commit a sexual assault.

Rape ironically is more mental than physical. I didn't know it then, but my family members tried to use sexual assault to maintain a psychological control over me. Little did I know that they would plan and try to continue their psychological advantage later in my life.

As I mentioned, I never told my parents. This fact ate at me later in my life when I had to face these emotions. I was constantly reminded of the sexual assault by symbols or by attorneys attacking the Boy Scouts in commercials for their sexual abuse of young boys. I wanted to hold my family members accountable. A simple, "I am sorry Ken for raping you" would quench my thirst for justice against these family members.

Unfortunately, I got no apology or even an acknowledgment of the awful act. If you think about the transgression and the response, it is deceitful and immoral. Where did my family members learn such immorality? I had not come close to such behavior and had only tried to better myself. Why would my family members try to tear me down instead of building me up?

The details of the rape played over in my mind constantly for the next few weeks. I could not shake the images out of my head as I had trained myself to do when I was younger. Why did they rape me? In some odd way, I think it was a punishment for being such a good son to my father.

I lost something that day. Although I made up for the indiscretion forced upon me, I never was the same. I know my confidence would never be the same after I was raped and sodomized by my family members. I will never know what the true cost of this rape would be on my life, but it was high.

More than fifty years have passed, yet my home at 100 Park End Place still feels like a crime scene rather than a warm colonial. Even to this day, when I walk into my parents' bedroom, I feel as if I am walking on evidence. The room where I played on my mother's stomach was now void of any cheer for me.

As I laid in my marital home in Ashland, Virginia my nightmare images wouldn't go away along with the howling of the owl and animals, I had to finally confront my childhood trauma. I was married to Janet for over 30 years and I had not even shared this with her. The most haunting image for me, was the jar of Vaseline. Every time I see a jar of Vaseline in the store or at home, it makes me cringe. It is the symbol imprinted in my mind of my sexual assault. I never got therapy to deal with the nightmares as I thought I was tough enough to shut it out. Shutting out the emotions of the rape required me to just not feel any emotions during bad times. It was a control mechanism that worked for me during my young adult years and during my career. I could be happy and enjoy laughter with relative ease. However, during bad times, I was emotionless, and I couldn't feel the emotions to cry. I felt sad, but no tear would emerge from my eyes. I just chalked the lack of tears up to being tough.

Later in life, on my father's death bed, he would say, "I want to thank you for setting a role model for your family members." Then he looked me in the eye and said, "But don't expect them to thank you for it." My father's words were profound and would be prophetic after his death. I thought of his words as a warning. I just wish he had warned me about fifty years earlier so I could have avoided my first tear.

10

MEETING MY WIFE

UPON ARRIVING AT FAIRFIELD, I immediately knew I was different than most of the kids. My clothes were different, and I did not have any of the preppy clothes the kids wore. I never knew kids who wore boat shoes or argyle sweaters. My roommate was a Grateful Dead fan, and I had never heard any of this music. My roommate rarely spoke to me and clearly, he was uncomfortable with our living arrangement. I lived in Regis Dorm, and I was the only Black student on my floor. Some kids had famous dads like the Mara kid, whose father owned the New York Giants, and the Donovan kid whose father was Secretary of Labor. I got along great with the kids on my floor, and my freshman year went by fast, and I did well academically.

Basketball, on the other hand, was a difficult transition. The guys were much bigger than me, and my body was not ready to play Division 1 basketball. I rarely played my freshman season, and I was miserable.

Socially, there was not much Black culture at Fairfield University in 1978. All the Black students ate at one table in the cafeteria, and there were a few Black girls. I became friends with Johanna Warner from Mount Vernon, New York, and we studied a lot together. Johanna was a big flirt and teased me often about getting together and coming over to her room. She was a Caribbean girl who came from a strict family, and she did not have any serious inclination of having sex. I never figured Johanna out my freshman year. Either she was immature, or she was a professional tease. After my freshman year, I left Fairfield University with a burning desire to improve upon my body for basketball and to improve my social life on campus.

As soon as I got to campus my sophomore year, Coach Fred Barakat called me into his office and told me he was moving me to the Far East dorm to room with Flip Williams. Coach Barakat thought it might help me transition to be a better basketball player by having a basketball player as my roommate. I was glad to move from Regis dorm as I did not have much in common with any of the guys or any social connection. Flip was from Neptune, New Jersey, but he had acclimated to the White New England culture well as a junior. Flip was also a confident person and basketball player. I learned a lot from him on the basketball court. Although Flip was Black, we had little in common. He was an only child from an upper-middle-class family and was very reserved. He also had an affinity for dating White girls, and he would constantly bring his White girlfriend, Becky, to our room. One-night, Flip mentioned that a family friend had enrolled at Fairfield and his mother was bugging him to show her around. Sensing his frustration with this situation, I asked him what her name was, and Flip responded, "Janet Norman from Belmar."

Jokingly, he said he should invite her over so I could meet her. I did not answer but just sat in my chair and rolled my eyes. Flip and I got along well together as my study habits rubbed off on him and his social habits rubbed off on me. At least he was a big improvement from my freshman roommate Ray. Our room was the hot spot for social interaction in the Far East dorm with lots of different types of people. This was all attributed to the popularity of Flip. Finally, one day Flip came into the room disgusted and frustrated. I asked, "What's wrong?"

He replied, "Janet from Belmar is coming over in a few minutes."

It got quiet between the two of us and then there was a knock on the door. Flip opened the door and in walked Janet Norman from Belmar, New

Jersey. Janet was a light-skinned Black girl that was mixed and had the preppy look mastered down to the boat shoes. Her clothes were baggy, and she had a very unassuming disposition, but she was cute and attractive. Flip introduced us and tried to make some small talk to facilitate a discussion. Pretty soon it got quiet in the room, and Janet just started crying. I looked at Flip, and Flip looked at me. I thought to myself what the hell is going on. I felt sorry for the girl. She started sobbing and saying, "I don't know anyone here." She started to explain that the girls on her floor were not very nice to her.

Recognizing Flip's hesitancy to get involved in the situation, I chimed in, "Don't worry. It's going to be okay."

I explained to her how rocky my freshman year went and the difficulty I had bonding with my freshman roommate and the guys on my floor. Janet smiled at me and a sense of calm came to the room. Recognizing her vulnerability, Janet quickly tried to exit the room. I said, "Hold on. Let me walk you home."

She waited and said, "Okay."

Flip smiled at me and looked relieved to pass his problem over to me.

Janet and I walked slowly in the dark and up the hill from Far East dorm to her Gonzaga dorm. At first, we did not have much to talk about, so I asked about her friends and boyfriend at home. She brightened up as she talked about her sister and her best friend Laura. Then she became sullen as she mentioned her boyfriend Steven had not contacted her since she moved on campus. She quickly rambled out that Steven was an army cadet at West Point and that they had a very serious relationship. Trying to calm her, I said, "He is just busy, and you'll hear from him real soon."

She smiled at me again and said, "I hope you're right."

By this time, we were in front of Gonzaga's dorm and Janet thanked me for walking her home. We shook hands and said good night and I fast-walked back down the hill to the Far East dorm.

In retrospect, I think my future wife was clever to get Flip and me to bow to her emotions. After that first night, Janet came to our room every night whether Flip was there or not. At first, I just thought she was lonely, and her family told her to look up to Flip as a mentor and resource. I walked her home every night and she would talk about her boyfriend Steven primarily. In the beginning, I was not attracted to Janet, and I was just being a gentleman by walking her home.

One-night Janet came over, and I had Lois from Bridgeport visiting me and it made for quite an awkward evening. Lois was a sexy urban girl from Bridgeport that I met from my classmate Vinny Jarvis. Lois in some ways reminded me of Kathy from East Orange because she was sexy and fun, but we had little in common intellectually or emotionally. Janet stayed the whole night with Lois and me. She finally left when I had to take Lois home.

Janet started to meet other people as she came to our room and she met Renee from the Far East dorm. Renee was a sexy Brooklyn girl and very outgoing. She took Janet under her wing and they became good friends. I did not pay much attention to Janet during her visits to our room. She was always wearing baggy preppy clothes that did not do her figure any justice. After she started hanging with Renee her look started to change, and she started wearing more form-fitting clothes that pronounced her figure. Janet from Belmar was a hottie hiding under those baggy preppy clothes. One sunny day, I was riding in my friend's truck down to the Far East dorm. Standing outside in a beautiful blue dress with her firmly shaped thighs and legs was Janet. I said wow to myself and as we passed by, I brashly said to Janet, "If you keep wearing those dresses, I might have to pay you a visit."

As we slowly passed, she flashed me a big smile, and I instantly felt a new connection to her. Looking to make a social connection on campus, I started to visit Janet in her dorm room. She had a weird roommate, Susan from Massachusetts that had an eating disorder, anorexia. Susan as a freshman was engaged to some rich man from Boston and would vomit her food regularly to keep herself in an extremely thin shape. The relationship between Janet and Susan was strained so Janet looked to get away from her dorm as much as possible. Little did Janet know that every season the basketball team had a dinner party where you could invite a date. I was sizing up Janet to take as my party date when one day Amelia Lopez said hello to me. Just that quick, as I learned in high school, love can be complicated.

Amelia Lopez was from New Haven, Connecticut, and she was flat out gorgeous but quiet. For Amelia Lopez to say hello was a big deal. Soon thereafter, I started speaking to Amelia, and I was tempted to ask her to the basketball dinner party. What a dilemma? Janet was the cute, smart preppy girl while Amelia was the Puerto Rican dime that every guy wanted. To be quite honest, I was intimidated by Amelia and was afraid to ask her to the party. My confidence during my first two years at Fairfield University was not very high. I was afraid to ask Amelia and be rejected. In Janet, I felt I had the safe bet and we got along well.

In retrospect, playing it safe was a trend in my life and career. Later, I would regret playing some of my professional decisions safe as I probably did not reach my full professional potential. I asked Janet to the party, and she said yes. It was our first formal date, and it started a journey that would bear two lovely kids and many great memories. Fairfield University, although not perfect for me, allowed me to blossom as a man and meet my wife of 30 years.

I loved my wife and although I was an imperfect husband, I was always there for her. I supported her emotionally and financially when her business struggled. I can remember when her business almost failed and she was depressed. I went and bought her a small blue vase that read "HOPE." I remember telling her that whatever the circumstances, there always was hope.

Janet was a good engineer, and she devoted a substantial amount of time and resources to developing her firm. In retrospect, this was probably the first crack in our marriage as Janet never visited me at my job for lunch or had much energy for fun after work. We did meet after work every day for dinner and to meet up with friends. Janet craved the social interaction brought by our Richmond, Virginia, social group. I, on the other hand, could take it or leave it from the Richmond buppies we came to know as "so-called" friends. This was probably the second crack in our marriage as Janet rarely wanted to be home alone. After some time, she always wanted to go out with friends, and this bothered me very much. Janet and I had an active sex life and we made love frequently. I can remember talking with her about our sex life and she said to me, "Ken when I am with you, I always feel love."

However, I think our sex life was the third crack in our marriage as I never felt emotionally attached to my wife while making love. It was like she was somewhere else while we had sex. Maybe this is natural after making love to the same person after thirty years and maybe I was guilty of not keeping our sex life fresh. Although our marriage lasted 30 years it was not built on a strong foundation and was destined to have problems.

One problem with my marriage to Janet was we got married at a very young age. I was 25 and Janet was 24. Looking back, I can see how naive we were about the challenges of starting our careers, a family, and the pursuit of happiness. However, in my eyes, we had 29 good years and 1 very bad year. I truly believe if I could ignore that last year with my illness that Janet and I would still be married.

Our pursuit of marriage started around 1982. Janet had just graduated from the University of Connecticut, she was in a joint degree program between UCONN and Fairfield University in engineering and quickly started working at an engineering firm in New Haven, Connecticut. I had just finished my master's degree at the University of Connecticut and started the Ph.D. program in economics.

I was living in Storrs, CT, with Mike McKay. Mike was a former University of Connecticut basketball star and later played semi-pro basketball in the Continental Basketball Association. Mike and I got along great. We had fun hanging out in Willimantic, Connecticut, at the grungy bars. We also talked a lot about old rivalry games between UCONN and Fairfield University. We had a lot in common, and I was comfortable in Storrs with no reason to leave.

On weekends, I would go visit Janet in New Haven, and she had a nice apartment in West Haven close to the Long Island Sound. Janet and I dated steadily from my graduation from Fairfield straight through her graduation from UCONN. We had one break up during our UCONN days but quickly got back together. Things were going smoothly between Janet and me. We had a nice cohort of friends in New Haven. They were primarily Janet's friends from her engineering firm and some close friends from Fairfield and UCONN.

Life was pretty good as we had jobs, money, and friends to share our success. I was content dating Janet, but she was getting uneasy about our long-term commitment. One day on my visit to her in New Haven, she started a conversation about getting engaged with the intent of getting married within a year. I was completely blindsided by the conversation and had not given the thought of marriage any serious consideration. How could I be married and finish my Ph.D. program at the same time? I traveled back to Storrs with a lot on my mind. Thinking out loud I was asking myself, "Do I love Janet enough to marry her? What would my life be like as a married man? Was I ready for such a commitment?" These were tough questions, and I did not have the answers.

When I got back to Storrs, I had a long conversation with Mike McKay. Mike was a big guy about 6'6" with long arms and legs. But Mike had a severe mouth disease that left his mouth a little disfigured, and he had some preliminary surgery to correct his mouth and speech. I mentioned this because a lot of people thought Mike was a dumb guy or just a dumb jock because of his mouth, but he was a smart guy and very intuitive. Mike grew up in the tough ghettos of Bridgeport, Connecticut, and he fought his way out of the ghetto becoming an all-state basketball player. He was probably one of the most well-known basketball players ever to come out of Connecticut, and I needed his wisdom to help me through a very important part of my life. Mike and I rented an upstairs apartment on Mansfield Road which was a busy road in Storrs, Connecticut. As I drove down Mansfield Road, I saw big Mike standing in front of his car. I quickly sped up and jumped out of my car and said, "Hey Mike, where ya going?"

He smiled as much as he could possible with his swollen mouth and said, "I am off to get some pizza at Tony's."

I quickly blurted out, "Can I come with you? I need to talk with you."

He said, "Sure. No problem KD."

I parked my car and jumped in Mike's car. Mike always kept his car squeaky clean and played his music loud. With the loud music pumping, he pulled onto Mansfield Road and screamed, "What's up KD! I missed you."

Sarcastically, in my mind, I thought I did not miss Mike because he was hard to look at with his swollen mouth, but I replied, "Thanks bro' I missed you too."

Soon we pulled up to Tony's pizza which was the best affordable food in Willimantic and a clean watering hole for some cold beer.

Everybody knew Mike and loved Mike McKay because he was a UCONN basketball legend. As we walked in the owner said, "Hey big Mike. What can I get you?"

What service for two young Black men in the early 1980s. When I was with Mike, we were treated like royalty. Looking at me, Mike said, "Hey KD, what you want? I got you."

Mike was a cool dude, and I could not wait to talk with him. I said, "Pizza and beer will do."

Mike yelled to the owner in his majestic way, "Give me a large pizza and two beers!"

As Mike turned around, I could tell he was in a playful mood and he loved to joke around. In his Bridgeport slang, he said to me, "Killer KD back home. What have you been up to brother?"

I then got serious and said, "Mike, I got a problem."

Mike looked at me and grinned, "Yo, killer KD, you smart as hell. You ain't got no problem you can't figure out."

I said, "Mike, this is serious. I need you to focus, man."

Mike gave me a long stare and jokingly said, "Oh shit KD, you serious. What ya got?"

I started to explain to Mike that Janet wanted to get engaged and get married in probably a year. Mike looked at me and said, "Don't do it KD."

I trusted Mike's instincts because he was a mature Black man that made it out of the ghetto with literally nothing, but his bare hands and his hands were massive. Letting Mike's answer sink in, I asked Mike, "How can you answer so quickly Mike?"

Mike said, "KD, I have been living with you for almost a year, and I never hear you talk about this woman. KD, all you talk about is economics and finishing your Ph.D." He continued "Now you're gonna let this woman step in front of your dream. If it was me, I wouldn't do it KD."

Mike had made a good point. The Ph.D. program in economics was rigorous at UCONN. More importantly, I was captivated by the math, logic, and creative stimuli I got from the people and the department. Focusing back on Mike, I said, "But Mike, I love her."

Then Mike gave me his insightful answer, "Hmm, what's love got to do with it and what is she doing for you?"

At this point, I did not have an answer for Mike. The pizza was delivered to our table and it was smelling good. I said, "Thanks Mike," and I picked up a juicy, greasy slice of Tony's pizza and gobbled it down.

Deciding on whether to marry Janet or not would have to wait. Mike and I continued to laugh and reminisce about basketball in the Big East while drinking our beer and finishing the pizza. I felt relieved that the question of marriage floated away as a distant memory.

Mike and I drove back to the house and decided to go out on the town that night to have some fun. Most of the bars of any size were in Willimantic, Connecticut, and Willimantic was an old mill town that used to be the "thread city "of the world. All the mills have since closed in Willimantic, and it was an earthy midsize town with an eclectic population of Whites, Blacks, Puerto Ricans, and many other ethnicities. This eclectic vibe made Willimantic a fun city to party in as there were many kinds of women always out partying. You must remember, we were young, looking for fun, and dumb.

Mike and I went out to the Dean's Office club that night in Willimantic looking to have some fun and get my mind off marriage. Mike was instantly recognized as his large 6'6" inch frame glided into the club. I followed Mike and found a nice quiet spot off to the side of the dance floor. I never knew it, but in hindsight, Willimantic had some fast women that were into all kinds of things. As I mentioned earlier, the city was in a steady decline since the disinvestment of the thread industry. Many families and men in Willimantic were heroin addicts, drunks, and many other garden variety drugs and vices.

I got to know one sweet lady from Willimantic named Evelyn, and she was a beautiful light-skinned Puerto Rican but built thin. Evelyn was the janitor at one of the buildings on the UCONN campus, so we talked now and then. I was attracted to Evelyn, but I never dated her, but we would always flirt with each other heavily. Later, I would learn that Evelyn was a heroin addict. Well ironically, Evelyn was at the club with a bunch of her girlfriends dancing freely out on the dance floor. I noticed Evelyn, and she noticed me. She walked over to me with her friend and said, "Hey Kenny. What are you doing here?"

I quickly replied I was just getting out of the house. Evelyn's friend wasn't paying any attention to us, but Evelyn bumped her and said, "Barbara, this is Ken. Can you two chat? I have to go to the bathroom."

We both nodded our heads over the loud music and Barbara smiled at me.

Suddenly, a song came on by Toto called *AEIOU and Sometimes Y*. It was a catchy dance song and Barbara said, That's my jam! " You wanna dance?"

I answered, "Sure."

Barbara and I hopped on the dance floor and danced to a few songs. Barbara was a good dancer, and she moved in a hypnotic trance as if she were on some psychedelic drug. I did not think much of the dance at the time as I was not a good dancer or a real party guy. However, the image of Barbara stuck in my mind. Barbara was a cute French-Canadian woman whose father was a hard-working plumber in the city of Willimantic. She was a little rugged, but she was cute, energetic, and fun. After dancing, she pulled me over to the side and started some heavy flirting with me. Looking me straight in the eye she said, "You know you want some of this."

Now I remind you, I was just coming out with Mike to get my mind off marriage. I had no intention of hooking up with a French-Canadian cutie from Willimantic. Also, keep in mind, I had never dated interracially and was only familiar with my roommate Flip's affinity for White women. This was new territory for me, but I was intrigued, and Barbara was persistent. Evelyn never came back as she was probably getting high on heroin in the bathroom. Barbara danced around me all night and whispered sexy thoughts to me that I had not heard from a woman.

I looked over at Mike by the bar, and he was smiling from ear to ear. He was surrounded by an all UCONN clan who were peppering him with old UCONN game questions. As I zeroed back in on Barbara, she was drunk but still dancing around me. She smiled at me and said, "I'm with my girlfriends, so I won't go home with you, but I'll give you my number."

She slowly danced off to write her number on a napkin then swiveled back over to me and stuck her number in my pocket. Smiling like Cinderella

Meeting My Wife

running away, she said, "You better call me."

I smiled, kind of not knowing what to make of the encounter. I was excited but confused about my relationship with Janet. Looking over at Mike, he gave me the signal we should leave, and we walked to the car to go home. Grabbing me by the neck, he said, "You ain't getting married boy. She was all over you."

Smiling in a boyish manner, I said, "No joke."

Willimantic had lived up to its reputation as a wild party city for my night, and it could have consequences for me as I contemplated marriage over the next few months.

The following week, I went back to New Haven to see Janet. You have to remember this was the early 1980s, there were no cell phones, and speaking by telephone was relatively expensive given the modest income of a graduate student and a junior engineer. Janet and I spoke on the phone about once a week, but we didn't have constant communication given her busy job and my rigorous study schedule.

Our weekend get-togethers were the time that we showed our affection and voiced our views, opinions, and desires. This weekend, Janet was on a mission to make it clear that she wanted a long-term commitment from me, and I had to make a choice. She was not going to be led down an empty street and have me leave her without any future opportunity. I do not know if Janet had any other suitors, but she was hell-bent on forcing my hand.

To be clear, Janet was not making me marry her. I had the opportunity to say no, and she would have gone her way, but I did love Janet. I did not want to lose her. We spent the week walking by the Sound and eating at Jimmie's Seafood, a popular West Haven eatery. I now had some clarity on what I needed to do as my future was on the line. I drove back to Storrs a little more relaxed because my relationship with Janet was growing, and we were in love.

The drive from New Haven to Storrs was about an hour. It became more cumbersome once you got past Manchester, and you had to drive on the old Route 44 or Route 6. Both routes were dangerous and required full attention. The road, in a funny way, gave me some relief from thinking about my dilemma. I just drove thoughtlessly until I ended up in the driveway of my

Storrs apartment. I arrived home early Sunday evening as I did not want to drive on the dark, funky, country roads.

I looked forward to seeing Mike, and as I opened the door, who do you think I saw? Sitting in our living room talking to Mike was Barbara, the cute French Canadian. I blushed walking into the room and Mike was just grinning with glee. Not knowing what to say, I said, "How is everybody?"

Barbara was wearing some short shorts which accentuated her buttocks and she replied, "I'm fine."

Thinking to myself, I thought, "Yes, you are a fine little number."

Barbara continued, "I was driving up the road and saw Mike, so I dropped by to say hi."

Barbara was an aggressive woman who knew what she wanted. Mike sensing her intentions said, "Let me leave you two to talk," as he winked at me upon leaving the room.

Barbara chimed in, "I thought you lived here with Mike, and I wanted to see you." She continued, "Plus, you never called me."

I did not know what to think of Barbara, but I was glad to see her. In some way, she made things easy. She was a hard-working woman who was a receptionist at the local dentist. She was no dummy, and she was not a floozy. She was just free with what she wanted. In some ways, I was jealous of her freedom. I had a rigorous schedule of teaching and research that demanded a strict, disciplined approach. In some weird way, Barbara gave me some relief from this academic bondage.

Eventually, Barbara and I became good friends, and she would come over to the apartment often after her job. We made love abundantly and freely. She loosened-up my personality and got me to smoke weed. Before Barbara, I was a stuffed shirt, and after Barbara, I was a tie-dyed t-shirt. She pumped life into me, but I was unsure of committing her. The main reason was I was not quite comfortable dating interracially.

In the early 1980s, interracial marriage was not universally accepted, especially in East Orange, New Jersey. Second, I was afraid of getting stuck in Willimantic, Connecticut. Willimantic was a community that sucked your spirit dry in the early 1980s. I did not study all these hours to get stuck in Willimantic and get Barbara pregnant. Lastly, I was not in love with Barbara.

She was a wonderful woman, but we were just so different from an intellectual standpoint. I had to cut this relationship with Barbara and move on with my life. If I did not make the hard decision now, I would lose Janet and be stuck in a very mediocre town.

One morning, I told Mike I was moving out and moving to New Haven. He shook his head and said, "I understand KD. I know you don't want to be here, and I'll miss you."

I said, "I'll miss you too man."

Mike and I had grown close almost like blood brothers. We did not say much after that. I packed up my things over the next few days and moved to New Haven on the weekend. Janet was happy to see me, and I committed to marrying her over the next couple of weeks. We were happy together, and I was not distracted by the eclectic Willimantic parties.

I got a job at the City of New Haven as a Business Development Specialist. It was decent money for an entry-level position, and I was able to put away some money to buy Janet a ring. We went ring shopping together, and she picked out the ring of her choice. It was a big moment for me, and I called my mom and dad to share the news. My father was excited while my mom seemed to be indifferent. Early one day, I picked up the ring without Janet's knowledge and made a nice little dinner for the two of us in our West Haven apartment. She came in from work after a long day and hugged me. I said, "I got a surprise for you."

I dropped on one knee and looked into her eyes and asked, "Janet Norman, will you marry me please?"

She answered, "Yes."

We kissed and had a nice dinner with conversations about our future and how I picked up the ring. We were excited about our future together as it seemed bright. We made passionate love after dinner and fell asleep together. I was finally home.

11

MY CHILDREN

BECOMING A FATHER is my greatest achievement. It was also one of the many good things that came from the union of Janet and I. I will talk about my kids in their chronological order just because that is how I remember their life and my experiences with them. Talking about Kirsten after Taylor does not diminish my love or respect for what she has become or accomplished. I mention this because she always felt that she got the short end of the stick when compared to her brother. She may have a point, as I always got my twin brothers hand-me-downs and was always compared to my twin brother. So, I may have had an unrecognizable bias as a parent. I was not a perfect parent, but I did the best I could with the training and resources I had at my disposal.

    I could talk about my kids for days, but I will try to stay relevant and present the challenges that I faced as a father. Taylor, who was adopted, is an outstanding young man and is now an actor in the traveling Broadway show, *Hamilton*. Kirsten is a beautiful young woman who takes her resemblance from my mother's side and the Taylor sisters from Luray, Virginia. My mother has a slew of sisters and they were all beautiful, especially my mom and Aunt Elaine. Kirsten is now a psychiatric nurse and will start her Ph.D. in nursing soon at John Hopkins University. Janet and I adopted Taylor after we could not bear children in the early years of our marriage. Janet was adopted by her parents, and we always talked about adopting a child before we got married. Adopting Taylor just came naturally, but as soon as we adopted Taylor, Janet got pregnant with Kirsten. In retrospect, this seemed like God's blessing for adopting Taylor as he denied us a child early on so we could nourish Taylor's gift to the world.

Taylor is quite the renaissance man, and I raised him with every benefit I did not receive as a young man. I wanted my kids to have only the best education and be thoroughbreds in their training. Early in my career, I learned that the quality of an education matters and sometimes you can be held back just because your schooling is perceived to be second class. For example, the University of Connecticut is excellent, but it is a few tiers below Harvard. There were many examples in my finance career, where no matter how hard I tried, my training was not sufficient to compete with the best from the top universities. I did not want my children to be held back by these institutional perceptions. My training from a satisfactory public-school system plagued me in higher education as I was not appropriately skilled in the fundamentals. Although I took advanced classes in high school, they still did not equip me to compete with the best students from the *best* high schools. These are just cruel facts, and I did not want my children to be at this competitive disadvantage. However, it would not be this simple and both of my children paid the price for the social mistreatment along with the subtle racism that they faced at the Collegiate School in Henrico, Virginia. Collegiate School is an upscale private school located just outside Richmond, Virginia, and is a first-class educational system from kindergarten through grade 12.

Both of my kids did their formal training at the Collegiate School, and it cost me a pretty penny. I say it cost me because my wife never cut one check for the Collegiate School. I paid for our kids' private school education and college by trading penny stocks along with taking loans against my secondary retirement account. Janet never understood the risk it took to finance our children's private education or college, nor do I think she cared, in retrospect. In hindsight, I think any activity which took more money away from me and towards the kids was just fine with her. Besides, Janet put all her resources into establishing her engineering firm, Daniels and Associates, which was her baby. In this sense, she prioritized her business and didn't contribute financially to the kids' educational activities as much as she should. Janet may not have financially invested in the kids properly, but she was emotionally vested in the kids and that may be as great as or greater than any financial investment.

On my end, the effort I put forth to give my kids an educational advantage was substantial and worth the price I paid. Early in Taylor's life, I recognized he had a gift for movement and dance. As an infant, Taylor would watch the complicated Barney cartoon dance moves and replicate them instantly, on the spot. It was quite impressive. This led to special early training in dance at the Pine Camp School of Dance under Ms. Holt, a legendary ballet teacher in the City of Richmond. This was followed up with dance training at the Richmond Ballet, a prestigious regional ballet company with an excellent reputation. All these special training costs money. Taylor also participated in many shows such as *The Nutcracker*, along with *Romeo and Juliet*, where he was a Black Romeo. The time and effort were enormous for Taylor because, in his early years, he was a little overweight and pudgy.

Taylor's success in dance was not an obvious or guaranteed achievement. However, I give myself some credit, because I saw my son's passion and his dedication to work hard. I believed in him and nothing could shake my admiration or determination to provide for his necessary training.

Training for Taylor continued as I put him in expensive gymnastics school. The time commitment became crazy as the gymnastic school owners used the parents as unpaid labor to run the gymnastic school bingo parlor. Taylor trained in gymnastics up to about a level 5 and was pretty good, but again I spared no cost to develop Taylor's ability. Next up for Taylor was Taekwondo, and he rose to black belt.

Probably the highlight of Taylor's training was the summer dance camp with the prestigious Alvin Ailey Dance Company at the age of 12. What Black father do you know searches out the best dance camps and enrolls his son in an expensive dance camp for the summer away from home? I still remember pleading with the director, Ms. Jamison, to let Taylor in the six-week camp even though he didn't meet the 13-year-old age requirement. The famous Ailey director was hesitant, but she acquiesced saying, "OK, let's see how he does."

Taylor was the only boy in the camp but danced circles around most girls, and they even did a special African dance rendition with Taylor as the lead. It was special, and I was a proud papa. Taylor and I bonded that summer as we lived together in New Jersey at my childhood house.

Over 18 years, Taylor evolved as an artist and a scholar with an awareness of his Black pride. Do not worry. We put in a lot of *no pressure* Father and Son time on the golf course or fishing.

I recall a conversation with one of the teachers at Taylor's preschool that stuck with me. The Head nun of Holy Angels preschool said to me, "Mr. Daniels, you're not like the other fathers. I watch how you talk to Taylor. You take the time to teach him and explain what he is supposed to do and how to act. The rest of these kids are just running around."

Her words immediately made me think of my father. My dad spent a lot of time being a great role model for me and did the best he could to help me succeed. He didn't have the resources to put me in a private school or to give me special training but he did give me his time. I especially remember a Father-Son baseball game in Washington Park where my father was there playing. I will never forget, as I was about 12 when my father took his turn at bat and hit a home run over the fence! Wow, that was my dad and I felt special! I wanted Taylor to feel special, and I used every opportunity I could to lift him.

Taylor excelled academically at the Collegiate School but struggled socially as he was one of the few Black kids in the class, and there were not any Black girls. As you can imagine, when it came time for dating, Taylor struggled to date any of the White girls although he tried and had many crushes on a few White girls. None of Taylor's attempts flourished into a relationship with a White girl at Collegiate School. I wondered if I had made the right decision for my son.

I would drive Taylor to school most of the time with Eric Williams' son, little Eric. Eric Williams was a senior executive at the American

Express Investment firm and Black. Eric's wife, Nyna was Indian and their union was unique given the Indian culture's racist disposition toward Black people. Nyna and Eric's union rose above this barrier and was exemplary. However, Eric Sr. did not escape racism as the good old boys of Richmond excluded him from the formal social circles even though he was their boss! He let Janet and I know that he was not fond of the "Richmond Way" as it was known.

In Richmond, if someone of a certain status did not know you then you must be introduced to that person by someone in his inner circle to receive the proper and formal attention. This was called the Richmond Way. Racism was rampant in Richmond, Virginia, for the children and the adults. I also experienced severe racism at Virginia Commonwealth which we can explore later. Taylor also experienced racism in the classroom at the Collegiate School as the young teachers played favoritism to the rich White parents. I always had to be on high alert at the parent-teacher conferences to defend Taylor's rights but also to diminish any damage the racist overtones could impress on my son.

As a father, I do not know if I was always successful in eliminating the negativity of the Collegiate School social scene on Taylor. Taylor had many guy friends and was well-received at the wealthy homes of his Collegiate buddies. I will admit that I was concerned that Taylor was enamored with the wealth and the materialism of the upper-class *Richmonders* but this was the price to pay to be exposed to the best education available. In retrospect, it was a difficult trade-off.

Probably, the most difficult day I had as a father was the day, I learned that Taylor was gay. I still remember the day my son came home and told me he was gay. I did not receive the message well and I seemed to be the only one in the house who he did not tell. It started with Taylor's senior speech, which every senior at the Collegiate School must give, as a coming-out speech. The word got around that Taylor was gay. Although Taylor didn't explicitly say he was gay during the speech, he hinted that he was torn about his sexuality and how to express it. I give my son credit that he had the conviction to follow his truth and express his sexuality to his Dad openly. At first, I flew off the handle and kicked Taylor out of the house as a sign of my dissatisfaction and leverage to maybe change his mind. I had no leverage, and Taylor left willingly without voicing any displeasure towards me.

Janet even supported my action to kick him out of the house. My daughter Kirsten, however, was visibly upset with me and expressed herself strongly. She said while crying, "Daddy, how can you kick Taylor out of the house?" She then continued rising in tone, "It doesn't matter if Taylor is gay," and she concluded with a hiccup cry, "You are supposed to love him no matter what."

In just a few emotional moments, my daughter had stripped me bare as a lousy father and a bigot towards homosexuality while showing no empathy for my son's plight. What is ironic is that I had plenty of gay friends and colleagues who I supported openly without bigotry. My close family friend, Thenois, is gay and we have been friends since childhood. I openly embraced Thenois and his sexuality. Janet's engineering friend, Charles, is gay, and I thought nothing of his sexuality. On the other hand, maybe I was not embracing homosexuality properly or in a comprehensive wholesome way that was authentic. I was not gay and it was hard to embrace my gay son. I viewed it as a rejection of my teachings and viewpoints. This was a selfish act, and I had to correct it quickly

Kirsten was still in her room sobbing when I walked in and I tried to comfort her. Speaking softly to her I said, "Little Miss, you know I love Taylor, and I was wrong."

She looked at me sobbing and said, "I want Taylor home."

Supporting her view, I said, "You're right Kirsten. We need to get Taylor back home."

I hugged her and walked down the stairs to talk with Janet.

Walking up to Janet in the kitchen, she was busy making some food on the stove and never stopped to look at me or acknowledge my presence. Keeping my distance, I asked, "So how long did you know?"

While multi-tasking she said, "I have known for quite a while as Taylor was struggling with how to tell you."

I did not know whether to be angry that Janet did not tell me that our son was gay or to thank her for handling the situation properly. I don't think I would have exploded with emotion if I had known my son's secret but I was blind-sided by the decision to not tell me. His sexual identity had many ramifications for my family. Janet finally stopped cooking and looked at me and said, "Well, we knew you weren't going to take it well, so Taylor and I decided not to tell you."

I said, "Hell! How did you expect me to react?"

Janet then firmly said, "Ken, you can't make the boy be something he's not."

I stepped back from Janet and sat down at the kitchen table by the bay window overlooking my yard. My mind wandered to the yard and my plants: my peonies, my astilbe, my viburnum, my lavender, my lamb's ear, and my sedum. Then it hit me. Taylor was not mine. I do not mean he was not my son because he was adopted. I meant that Taylor was not mine to possess like a plant or a car, or a house. Taylor was a human being, free to be whomever he desired to be and free of any restriction that I or society wanted to place on him. My yard was mine now and needed me for nourishment to thrive. Taylor did not need me anymore for nourishment. I had guided him and trained him to be an independent thinker who could create his destiny. Yes, he would benefit from my fatherly love and I would be there for him, but the overweight, pudgy boy was now a 6'3" muscular young man with ambition.

Falling back into the kitchen, I said to Janet, "Let's go bring our baby boy home."

In a tender moment, she walked over to me and put her hands on my shoulders, and said, "He will always be your boy."

Quickly I said, "So, where is he?"

Janet then began to explain that Taylor was at the house of a teacher from Collegiate and would be spending the night. She then explained that we should probably let things settle down, and she would give Taylor a call in the morning.

I was mentally exhausted as I got up from the table and said, "Okay."

I then walked back upstairs and tapped on Kirsten's door. She said, "Yeah."

I poked my head in the room and said, "Taylor's coming home tomorrow."

"Are you sure?" she asked.

I replied, "I'm sure. So, no more crying. Okay?"

Unconvinced, she responded, "Okay."

Feeling a little better about my emotions, I walked towards my bedroom and plopped down on the bed. I didn't even take my clothes off. I fell asleep easily and did not even remember Janet getting in the bed. I woke up the next morning feeling like I had a bad dream.

You must remember, I was a scholar-athlete who ate and slept basketball. Most of my basketball friends pushed their kids, boy or girl, into competitive sports. I took a different approach, and let Taylor choose his passion and supported it unconditionally. I was not naive about homosexuality and dancers. I knew a good number of dancers were gay. I was just praying that Taylor would be different and would set a new standard for the industry and himself. I was wrong, and now I had to face my son and our new norm.

Rolling over in the morning, I nudged Janet in the bed and said, "It's time."

She said, "Give me a minute."

She eventually called the teacher and we were set to meet Taylor at noon in the parking lot by Panera Bread not far from our house.

I anxiously awaited the meeting with Taylor. It seemed like it took forever for noon to come around. I walked my ten-acre lot and picked over my plants and picked out weeds. Finally, 11:45 rolled around, and everyone at the house loaded into our blue Suburban. Panera Bread was right down the hill, just a short ride from our house. Janet and Kirsten were completely quiet during the ride, and I turned on the radio to mute the silence. We pulled into the shopping mall parking lot and waited for Taylor. Soon a car pulled up, and Taylor popped out and jumped into the back seat with his sister. I started the conversation and everyone listened intently. It was probably the most emotional time in my life, and I am glad that I was able to cry. What a relief to feel the tears come down my face. I still had some emotional humanity as I cried for the second time in my life. The first time was when I was raped by a family member as a nine-year-old kid.

No Tears

Looking at Taylor, I said, "Son, I'm sorry I didn't listen to you, and I overreacted. Please accept my apology."

I could tell Kirsten and Janet were pleased with my initial introduction but remained quiet and tuned in to my appeal. Next, I said, "Taylor, I don't care if you are gay. I am just concerned for your well-being because the world is not yet fully accepting of gay men. I just don't want to see you get hurt."

This was the year 2008, and homosexuality was an evolving movement gaining more acceptance year by year. However, in Richmond, Virginia, the culture was very conservative and most gay men did not openly flaunt their sexuality.

It was at that point that I just burst out crying. Kirsten followed my crying and even Janet could not hold her tears. Kirsten hugged her brother and Taylor joined the family cry as we cleansed the moment with some authentic tears of family love. I will never forget that moment in our Suburban. It was the most touching family moment in my life. Looking back, it has a special meaning, since, in about eight more years, I would lose my formal family unit after the divorce.

I finished my appeal by saying, "I love you son."

Taylor remained quiet while I spoke but looked me in the eye to gauge my sincerity. Next, Janet affirmed my position. She said, "Your father's right. The world is a very cold place and we want you to be happy."

Taylor finally spoke up and said, "I know who I am, and I will find a way to make it in this world."

My son was ready to leave the nest. Although I wanted to provide more guidance to Taylor, it was not needed. He was mentally mature and confident beyond his years. In some ways, his confidence surpassed mine as Taylor was taught to never settle for anything less than a top-shelf   . I started up the Suburban and started on the way home. Janet looked at me but did not say a word. Taylor and Kirsten quickly fell into some idle chit chat and laughter. Our new norm came chaotically but quickly calmed down to a peaceful openness of truth. Now the truth, out of the darkness, provided some sunlight along with a cleansing and a chance to start anew. I still had some reservations about the impact of Taylor's decision on the family but my grip at the helm could no longer be held together by position. My family was changing before my eyes, and there was nothing I could do to stop it.

A father and a son relationship evolves and can be like a love-hate relationship. I loved my father but hated to fall victim to his stereotype of me being beaten out by White boys. His favorite statement to motivate me was, "Wait until you get to Fairfield. Those White boys are going to kick your ass."

Sometimes my dad would say, "You think you know everything. Those White boys are gonna kick your ass."

As you can imagine, I hated these words and was determined to prove my father wrong. I never motivated Taylor with challenges. I motivated Taylor with tough love and opportunity. In some ways, this is just as challenging as my father's vocal threats. Taylor on the other hand had no reason not to succeed. All he had to do was prepare, show up, and perform. This is much harder than it seems and sometimes Taylor hated my control of the opportunity. Taylor was tired of my button-pushing on what was to come next. He wanted control of the opportunity whether it was his sexuality or his choice of school.

My means to make things happen were still needed for the next four years as Taylor prepared to go off to New York University. In New York, he would cultivate some more distance between us as he discovered his new norm. I told my son I loved him every chance I got, and he told me he loved me because he had nothing else to say. My mission for developing Taylor was accomplished. Now it was time to sit back and watch the show.

Although Taylor was a well-mannered young man, he had a sense of entitlement and never fully understood the degree of sacrifice necessary to put him through private school and NYU. I vividly remember asking Taylor to say thank you for his college education as he never told me to thank you after graduation or any formal or informal discussion. One conversation with Taylor went like this "So Taylor don't you think you should thank your father for putting you through NYU so that you have no debt". "Can't you say thank you." A few moments of silence passed. Taylor finally blurted out very casually, "I appreciate it". This indifferent and callous attitude signifies the good and the bad in my son. Never in a million years would I not recognize my father's contribution to my success. In Taylor's eyes, I was just doing my job and it didn't deserve any special mention. Such is the dilemma of raising millennials where certain basic norms such as respecting your parents need to be taught while it was a learned trait during the baby boomer generation.

Our decision to put Kirsten in Collegiate School was not an easy one. Admission to kindergarten through 12th grade at Collegiate School is an extremely selective process. The selection spots for kindergarten at the Collegiate School cost about $19,000 and the spots filled up quickly as acceptance into the "Lower School" almost guaranteed admittance to the Middle School and High School if your kid could handle the workload. I always thought the workload for the kids in the Lower School at Collegiate was insane. Taylor handled the workload fairly easily, but the teachers gave Taylor a hard time all the time by nitpicking some trivial issue.

Having this experience, Janet and I wondered if Collegiate School was the right place for Kirsten. We struggled with the thought of having our kids in two separate school systems and needed to consider the fact that Kirsten would probably be the only Black girl in her class. Weighing the options, we decided to place Kirsten in Collegiate School as the better option than Richmond Public Schools or another private school system.

Kirsten, as a young child, was a rambunctious ball of the fight. Her mother said she was feisty because she worked up to the day she delivered. The delivery of my daughter Kirsten was a beautiful experience. When I saw her head pop out of her mother's uterus I was amazed. The birth of life is an amazing experience and should be experienced by every male if given the chance. Kirsten's birth however was coupled with some complications and she was placed in ICU as a precaution. Dr. Boone was our pediatrician and she caught Kirsten's medical condition and was able to right the ship with the appropriate antibiotics. Thank God they saved my Little Miss.

Little Miss is the nickname I gave Kirsten as she was a little woman that hung right with her older brother and protected him. She was a fighter. I remember a children's outing at the Holy Angels preschool and some little boy was torturing Taylor. All of a sudden Kirsten jumped up and pushed the little boy down and mumbled, "Don't you mess with my brother."

I think she was 6 years old at the time. I mention this because Kirsten was bright and filled with energy. Janet and I wanted to cultivate and channel this energy so that Kirsten could reach her full potential.

I must admit that I thought Janet should take a larger role in raising Kirsten since she was a girl. I had my hands full with Taylor but I wanted to provide the same opportunities to Kirsten that I provided for Taylor. Just as I watched Taylor, I noticed that Kirsten was athletic like her dad and was strong for her age. I would try to develop her strength in gymnastics and track throughout her childhood.

Initially, we followed the same path as Taylor and enrolled Kirsten in the Pine Camp for dance. This is where Kirsten came out holding the hand of some Black little girl, who happened to be Ryan Claytor. To this day Kirsten and Ryan Claytor are best friends. Janet cultivated the relationship and became good friends with Ryan's mom, Randy Claytor. This social circle turned out to be the primary social circle for Janet and Kirsten but I was less inclined to join this Richmond group and kept my distance.

The Claytors were great people, but they accumulated friends like widgets. We spent a lot of time with the Claytors and even did some fun boating down on Lake Gaston in North Carolina. These are memories that I cherish as the kids experienced tubing and boat riding, something I never did as a kid growing up in East Orange.

Although Vernon Claytor was a nice guy, I did not want to be a widget friend. Janet clamored to be a part of this group and fell right in line. In hindsight, I might have been better off falling into the Claytor gang as it would have helped my assimilation into Richmond. This is something that became more important to Janet than to me over time, and it drove a wedge in our relationship. Kirsten blossomed as a young girl with her newfound friend, and she was an outgoing student at Holy Angels preschool. I was very happy with her development, and she was a very happy child.

One of the things that I noticed as we started to raise Kirsten is that raising a girl is a lot of work and much more involved than raising a boy. First, girls have much more selection of clothes and you can spend much more money. The main issue with girls is their hair. Kirsten was a pretty girl and her hair was long but it was short compared to some of her girlfriends. Even Ryan Claytor had long silky hair, and this grew to be a competitive issue with the girls. This issue was magnified when we enrolled Kirsten in Collegiate School and the White girls came out with the super long hair. You could tell the girls were competing with their hair and when you watch the girls at an event, hair flipping was an art form. By the time Kirsten was in fourth grade, I could tell that this began to bother her.

Kirsten was keeping up with the workload in the Lower School, and I was proud of her. She was also making friends in the Lower School even though she was the only Black girl. Then the ugly head of racism reared its ugly head. To this day, I am pissed that I did not stop Ms. Bradshaw's treatment of Kirsten earlier. Ms. Bradshaw was a teacher in the Lower School and she was very Southern to put it lightly. I had no problem with Ms. Bradshaw's southern heritage, although the current Black Lives Movement would disagree with me. Southern heritage is an ugly memory in American history and should be taught as such. Ms. Bradshaw glorified southern history, but more importantly, she tried to imply that Kirsten could not do the work at an acceptable level for Collegiate School and was threatening to hold her back. At first, Ms. Bradshaw's bias slipped by me, but I picked up on her bias when Kirsten's demeanor began to change. She was no longer the rambunctious little girl and some of her energy had been zapped by Ms. Bradshaw's constant nitpicking of Kirsten's weaknesses without offering a strategy to help.

Enough was enough. We as parents went after Ms. Bradshaw at the parent-teacher conference. Ms. Bradshaw even had a condescending attitude towards us, but we cut through her southern pride to ask her why she was trying to hurt our daughter. Ms. Bradshaw, recognizing she was out on a limb, climbed back into a defensive position as she knew we would seek external action if she kept up her nonsense.

Kirsten's work miraculously improved after our parent-teacher conference, and we had no further problems with Ms. Bradshaw. Unfortunately, Kirsten's drive did not automatically bounce back as her confidence had taken a hit. The school year finally came to an end, and I was so glad to get my Little Miss away from Ms. Bradshaw. Kirsten matriculated to the Middle School at Collegiate and did well. It was when she entered the

High School where the social problems and subtle racism caused her to consider leaving the Collegiate School.

Kirsten had been the only Black girl at Collegiate through Middle School until two Black girls entered Collegiate School at the High School level. At first, I thought it was great that Kirsten had some Black girls that she could relate to and build some lifelong friendships with.

However, this is when the complaints started to escalate that the White girls were treating the Black girls differently. At first, the comments circulated quietly among the Black parents. In the entire high school, there were probably about 15 Black parental groups. As the complaints grew and needed to be addressed by the administration, and the administration tried to quell the concerns of the Black parents by hiring one of the Black parents as a diversity advisor. In my mind, this was a payoff to quiet the loudest complaining voices as the squeaky wheel always gets the attention.

Kirsten prospered in the High School academically and had regained her confidence and footing after the Ms. Bradshaw mishap. She was becoming a young woman and this is when dating was a desire in her mind and it was a problem at the Collegiate School. Taylor struggled with dating at the Collegiate School, as did Kirsten. The White boys were interested in her but they wouldn't formally date her and there weren't that many Black boys to make a considerable pool of choices. Kirsten had her good friend Ryan near home, but she was miserable socially at the Collegiate School. My desire to give her a quality education came with a huge penalty as I had great friendships from my High School and some of them are tight till today. Kirsten wanted to leave the Collegiate School although she was doing well academically. Janet and I had a serious discussion about coming up with a serious alternative for Kirsten's education. One day Janet and I at the dinner table discussed selling the house in Henrico County to move to a better school district. We lived in a nice brick split ranch in a predominantly Black neighborhood, Chamberlayne Farms, in Henrico County when Kirsten was a freshman. By the time she was a sophomore, we had put the brick split rancher on the market and was looking for a new house. I had done well at Virginia Commonwealth University (VCU) and had steadily gotten raises along with a promotion to Associate Professor so I felt confident we could make a move up in housing and keep the kids in private school.

At first, Janet and I focused our new house search in the West End of Henrico County as it was the fastest-growing area with the newest homes and the best schools. The new schools were beautiful campuses that would put many of the North East High Schools to shame. I thought back to my old high school which had been recently torn down because it was an old asbestos relic of the past. Most Black communities in the North East and in particular New Jersey were redlined into poor school systems that were separate and unequal to their White counterparts in the more affluent White communities. The Black Lives Matter movement of 2020 sought to capitalize on these legacy redlining cases in education, healthcare, and business. Janet and I did not want our kids to experience an inferior educational experience and we found that the city of Richmond and the Black neighborhoods of Henrico County had poor school systems. Looking at the West End schools, they just seemed like a larger more complex version of the Collegiate School system but they would be free.

However, we decided to continue our search looking for a better option. Janet and I liked to take Sunday drives and look at new houses or just drive and look around the new communities that were springing up in metropolitan Richmond. Richmond was a mid-size metropolis of the city of Richmond, Henrico County, and Chesterfield County. This geography encompassed about three-quarters of a million people and offered a sizable business opportunity for Janet's engineering firm and enough business activity that I had gotten placement on several prominent business boards. Things were looking good for the Daniels family but we needed to make sure our Kirsten had a good social environment. One day Janet and I drove out to Ashland and Hanover County. Although Ashland was a more central location than Hanover County, the fact is that Ashland calls itself the "Center of the Universe." Hanover County was starting to build some new schools and a new high school had just been built up the road on Route 301 from our current house. Janet and I decided to look and we were met with a pleasant surprise. The new Hanover High School was brand new with plenty of resources just like its Henrico County counterpart and it had a relatively more diverse student population. Now could we find a suitable house for the Daniels household that was within our budget? We continued driving around, actually got lost, and drove down a dead-end street. At the end of the street was a large 300-acre farm but adjacent to the 300-acre farm was a sale sign for Pulte Homes. However, there were no homes, only a trailer set to the side. We turned around and approached the trailer. As we pulled up to the trailer a young gentleman came out and said, "I'm Jim Ryan for Pulte Homes."

I responded, "Hi Jim, I am Ken Daniels and this is my wife Janet."

"Nice to meet you," said Jim and he continued, "What can I do for you?"

He went on to explain that Pulte Homes had purchased 300 acres of an old strawberry farm and due to Hanover County's 10-acre restriction they could only build 30 homes on the 300 acres. He said, "We have sold the first 28 lots and we have two 10 acre lots left that are just gorgeous."

In my mind, I thought, "Wow!"

I always wanted to own land and the location was perfect for Kirsten's schooling along with the commute for our jobs. Jim then asked if we wanted to see the two remaining lots and I said, "Of course."

We continued to briefly chat with Jim then hopped into our respective cars and followed him around the corner to a cul-de-sac street. We hopped out of the cars and Jim pointed to two thickly wooded lots across the streets from each other. He said, "Would you like to walk the lots."

I nodded my head, but Janet said, "I am not walking through the woods with the bugs."

Jim and I plodded through the thick trees of the pie-shaped ten-acre lot. It was massive for an urban kid who grew up in a congested environment. Finally, at the back of the ten-acre lot, Jim pointed to the boundary lines along with the streams and a beautiful cavernous gully with a small creek running through it. This was it. I was sold but the biggest surprise came when Jim pointed down a small hill to the left. Looking down was a small pond perfect for fishing. I was an urban kid, but I loved to fish. My mind quickly wandered off to a beautiful secluded home with bass fishing right behind the

No Tears

house. This would be my reality for a good portion of my life as I would teach both my kids to fish in the pond.

Fighting our way back out to the cul-de-sac, Jim and I found Janet patiently waiting. Excitedly, I said, "Jan, the lot is beautiful and there is a pond in the back."

Pulling Janet to the side, I started to explain to her the desirability of the 10 acres as an investment and its ability to solve Kirsten's new school problem. It did not take a lot to convince Janet that the new home lot in Hanover made sense for our future. Turning to Jim, I said, "We want the lot. What do we need to do?"

Jim explained that we needed a $500 check to hold the lot, and we could work out the contract details later.... what type of house did we want to build?

I didn't want to lose the lot so Janet and I drove straight home to get a $500 check and drove straight back to Hanover. Handing the check to Jim solidified my evolution and growth as a man as I took a substantial risk for me and my family with confidence. I did not waiver or consider that we could not pull off the substantial house upgrade and clear quality of life upgrade for my family. Quail Oak Court provided many years of happiness for the Daniels family and allowed Kirsten to leave Collegiate and attend Hanover High for her last two years of high school.

Kirsten's confidence as a young woman grew immensely as she entered her junior year. She was a beautiful young lady who was smart, strong-willed, independent, and ambitious. It was her independence that concerned me the most as a father. Kirsten could be aloof, and she could be "mouthy" at times as she would get her opinion across. I could tolerate independence, but I could not tolerate any disrespect towards me or her mother.

Kirsten and Janet started to bump heads and Janet tried to insert her will on Kirsten. Kirsten was just as strong-willed as her mother, and I would often step back to let the two ladies settle things. Thankfully, these blow-ups were relatively rare, but they symbolized the energy of Kirsten and her determination to give her input into any situation. Energy and independence are strong character traits and I looked to channel Kirsten's drive. Initially, gymnastics then track and field demonstrated Kirsten's drive. Then music

My Children

illustrated her talent and ambition. She was a beast at anything she put her mind to and it was fun to watch.

Kirsten entered Hanover High in her junior year and the transition was initially very smooth. Janet and I bought her a car, a cute used grey, 3-series BMW. It was a safe, reliable car. Her academics continued to be strong and she had a social life with some of the Black students at Hanover High School. Unlike Collegiate School, the socioeconomics was more varied and Hanover High School pulled students from every segment of society. Kirsten fit in well with her classmates and initially, she formed most of her friendship with girls. The girls seemed nice and Kirsten's social development seemed to be on track. She also now was in the same school district as her best friend, Ryan Claytors. This was the best outcome as Ryan was close but not in the same school. This gave Kirsten more of a foundation and she blossomed with confidence. She also ran the 440-yard race in track and field and showed some promise in the very competitive public-school conferences. I finally had my athlete, and I enjoyed the races. Kirsten's junior year pretty much went off as planned, and we seemed to be happy as a family.

Kirsten's senior year was a little rocky as she dated a few boys. However, none of the boys materialized into long term relationships and in hindsight that was a good outcome. Like me, she was free to leave Hanover with no commitments and find her dream.

Senior year for Kirsten went well academically, athletically, and she even branched out to the school choir. Boy could she sing. Trying to give Kirsten an opportunity, I called Kirsten's uncle who was a music producer and former performer in the group, *Surface*. Her uncle's nickname was Pickle, and he wanted to hear her sing. Pickle said, "Just call me on the phone and let her sing. I will tell you if she can sing."

I hung up the phone with Pickle with no expectation. I figured Kirsten would sing for her uncle and that would be it. One Friday after school, I called Pickle, and Kirsten sang for him over the phone. After singing for Pickle, Kirsten handed the phone back to me. I said, "Hey Pick. What's up?"

He simply said, "She can sing."

Pickle went on to explain that there was potential and that he would like to make an EP with her over the summer break. He would get the songs written and music produced. I would just have to pay for things at costs. In that short time span, I was turned into a music executive with my daughter as the star.

The following day I explained to Janet that Pickle wanted Kirsten to produce a few songs as an EP. Pickle lived in Montclair, New Jersey, so the project would require Kirsten and I staying at my childhood home for the summer. This was very similar to the experience I had with Taylor and the Alvin Ailey dance camp. I thought it was a great chance for me to bond with my daughter and a chance for Kirsten to spend some quality time with my mom, her grandmother. The time spent with my mom and dad was special for me, and Kirsten got to grow with my mom's tutelage.

Janet agreed to the project, and Kirsten and I spent the summer of her senior year recording an EP. The project worked out well as songwriter, K2 may he rest in peace, wrote some beautiful, catchy songs. The lead song was *Let Me See Your Cell Phone*. You can see the music video I produced of the song on YouTube.

Yes, following the completion of the recordings, I hired a videographer, and we produced a complete music video starring Kirsten. Taylor was in the video and showed off his future talent as a dancer. I had so much fun that summer. Pickle was the perfect host, and the project was a success. Although the project did not generate any significant revenue, Kirsten proved that she could prepare, perform, and execute. She was mature beyond her years and showed tenacity, drive, along with the ability to listen and adjust when directed. I was a proud father.

Kirsten enrolled in St. John's University that fall, and New York City was a big leap for her. As her father, I had concerns for her safety in New York City, but I had no questions about her ambition and her willingness to succeed. St. John's was perfect for Kirsten as it was a small cozy campus with Big City ambition. Kirsten excelled at St. John's and now my Little Miss was ready to ascend from the nest.

12

LOST SONS

I HAD ALWAYS WANTED a son that looked like me, talked like me, and had my distinct physical characteristics. What father doesn't? A biological son is one way that a man passes down his legacy, his wisdom, and traits to the next generation. This has been a generational passage dating back centuries for many different civilizations. Although a daughter can inherit her father's instincts and embody his ways, she cannot pass down the seeds of his legacy like a son. This is the cold biological truth. This was the dilemma I faced as I thought about the impact of abortion on my life and my legacy.

I love my son Taylor. He is everything I wanted in a son despite his decision to come out as gay man. I had reconciled with him to the best of my ability, and we had moved on. However, I could not quell the other demons in my life that peered their way into my head as I reconciled my life during my illness. There were two little dirty secrets that bothered me and the heartbeat of each got louder as I thought of the abortions. Yes, the abortions, plural. I had two pregnancies before marriage as a result of my reckless sexual behavior and I had impregnated each young woman accidently. I had proudly thought I had dodged a bullet with each one as I went off to fulfill my ambition and my dreams. Little did I know that each woman had a shocking message for me.

    I met Beth at the AEA summer program, and she was a different kind of Black girl that I had ever met. She attended Vassar University during the fall. Her behavior was prim and proper as she carried herself with an effortless level of class that exuded from her pores. She had a unique physique as she was slim but had a very busty chest that drew the eyes of every man who came near her. She was smart and funny, and we sat close to each other during the AEA summer program.

    I do not remember Beth and I hanging out that much during the summer of 1981. We were in a rigorous 6-week intensive economics program. The chances for a lot of social activity was almost nil. I do remember going to her room after dinner one night and kissing her. Our kissing quickly turned into heavy petting, and I made love to Beth. Beth was a beautiful dark skin Black woman whose dark skin radiated my soul. I was not attracted to White women, and I remember Beth's lovely dark skin as I put my lips on her dark skin. Sucking on her skin was almost like drinking dark chocolate milk and I loved some chocolate milk.

    The result of my sex with Beth got her pregnant and produced the seed of a child. How did I know Beth got pregnant? How did I know that Beth had an abortion?

    When we left the AEA summer program, Beth and I had decided to keep in touch. She lived in Mount Vernon, New York, and I visited her once in her oversized Colonial home. Mount Vernon was a predominantly Black suburb north of New York, and it was quite a distance from New Jersey. I never made it back to see Beth before the start of the fall semester, and I did not see her again until after I graduated from UCONN. Beth and I had lost contact with each other and moved on with our lives. I was working in New Haven after graduating from UCONN, and she was working in New York as an analyst. We accidently bumped into each other on the street near Central Park as I was visiting some friends that worked near Wall Street.

    My accidental meeting with Beth was awkward. She was still beautiful, her dark skin still radiated, and her breast still spoke directly to any man. We recognized each other immediately as she smiled at me. She said, "So Ken Daniels, what brings you to New York?"

I was happy to see Beth, and I wanted to learn about what she was doing professionally. I was curious if she kept in contact with anyone from the AEA summer program. I responded to Beth with some excitement and said, "Oh, I just visited some friends in the city. So, tell me what have you been up to?"

Beth began to tell me her activities upon her graduation from Vassar, and she was filling me in on her job activities when she suddenly stopped. She said, "Ken, I can't do this."

Curiously, I looked at Beth wondering what she was talking about. I looked at her eyes and saw a sadness had overcome her. She started to tell me what happened when she returned home from the AEA summer program in 1981.

Beth took her time and the tone in her voice changed towards me. It wasn't an angry voice but it was more of a voice of disappointment. She told a story of me abandoning her and leaving her alone to deal with her pregnancy. I was shocked as I did not know that Beth got pregnant from our encounter. Beth continued to explain that she tried to hide the pregnancy from her mother, but her mother eventually found out and demanded that Beth have an abortion so she could finish her senior year at Vassar. Standing in front of Beth I exclaimed, "Why didn't you tell me?"

Beth, frowning on her face, said with an intent to hurt, "Ken, you were very self-absorbed, and I knew you would find some submissive girl that you could manipulate".

Beth had made it clear that she was not happy that I got her pregnant, and then selfishly moved on without trying to climb the social ladder with her. In some ways, she was right, but I was being bombarded with a ton of information and trying to process what was being told to me. Beth continued, telling me that the aborted baby was a boy, and that she regretted the decision as she was Catholic. I stood in front of Beth wounded in many ways. We continued on with our conversation with Beth finishing me off with her final statement as she said, "Ken, I hope you grow up and become a mature man."

She gave me a quick grin or half smile and was quickly gone in the traffic of New York City.

What had just happened? Did I just get hit by a thunder bolt? I slowly gathered myself and meandered through the New York City streets to the subway. I sat on the subway and tried to recount my conversation with Beth.

Beth had just unloaded a whopper of a revelation to me. I had a son, and he was taken away. I did not know how to feel about the abortion. Did I dodge a bullet or lose someone special? At the time, as I rode the subway, I felt relief. I was dating Janet in the summer of 1981, and the news of a baby would have derailed our relationship and put my ambitious plans on hold. Had Beth done us a favor? I did not know the answer, and I never discussed the abortion with anyone. It was one of the many secrets I kept inside until my illness.

In retrospect, the abortion is something that I truly regret. As I mentioned earlier, it is the desire of every man to have a son. Janet and our union did not bear me the son of my dreams, so I felt cheated by Beth's singular action to abort our son. Just think, a little Kenny D was here and gone in a blink of an eye or more appropriately, gone with the cut of a knife. What could I have done differently?

Beth had made it clear that her decision was not an uninformed decision but a mature decision taking my undesirability into account. Given my immature or her self-absorbed description of me I was not a suitable mate or ready to be a father in her assessment. I tried to wrap my head around the decision but could not make any clear headway about anything. It was 30 plus years after the fact, but the beat of the heart still pounded in my ear. To make matters worse, there was nothing I could do to stop it.

The second abortion was with Janet and it was even more shocking as I had almost constant contact with Janet. Janet and I got to know each other in her freshman year and started dating in the later part of my sophomore year. According to Janet, she was a virgin in her freshman year and we initially made out and made love in my dorm room one day. We were attracted to each other but I don't remember us as having an active sex life or a lot of sex her freshman year. Her sophomore year was different as we both were more physically mature, and I remember us having a more active sex life. I was into Janet and we were growing closer. My junior year finished on a high note as Janet went home for summer, and I visited her as much as possible down in Belmar.

Towards the end of summer, I visited Janet and we went to the beach and held hands. We were having a good visit and returned to her home where she got into an argument with her sister. I was sitting in their living room as I heard the two banter back and forth. The sister proclaimed, "So you just think you are too good and you can do no wrong."

Janet, trying to calm the situation, bantered back, "What is your problem? Why don't you go somewhere?"

The sister insistent on escalating the confrontation said, "I bet Kenny doesn't know how good you are. I bet he doesn't even know about the abortion."

Suddenly my ears tuned into the conversation more acutely, and Janet didn't say anything and the sister continued to bark, "Oh, you mean he really doesn't know? I was just playing."

Janet left the room, and the sister slithered her way outside. I was now sitting in the room wondering what just happened.

Finally, Janet came back into the room with leftover tears in her eyes. I started by saying, "Is it true?"

Janet calmly said, "Yes, it's true."

She calmly started to tell me she got pregnant in the fall of my junior year, and that over the Christmas break her parents insisted that she get an abortion and not derail her studies. Once again, I fervently asked the question, "Why didn't you tell me?"

Janet said she was embarrassed and that her parents pretty much took control and guided the process. She even told me her account of her father driving her to the abortion clinic and how humiliated she was. Both of Janet's parents were nurses so I knew that the process of abortion for their baby girl had to be a difficult process. At first, I felt sadness for Janet and remorse for the baby, but then my response turned to anger. Directly confronting her I said, "How could you do such a thing without asking me?"

I felt betrayed by Janet even though I knew she had domineering parents. Didn't I have rights in the decision for our baby to live or die? Janet proceeded to explain that she did not have much choice in the matter although it was her body. I was disappointed in Janet's answer and I got in my car and drove back home to North Jersey.

During the drive up the Garden State Parkway, I had plenty of time to think of my lost child. Later on, I would learn that it was a boy that was aborted, and I had lost my chance at a son. Was I that reckless in my decision making that I was putting Janet, my future children and my dreams at risk? I never had to think of the consequences of my action in such dire terms as up to this point. I wasn't really sexually active and the hardest decision I had to make was to pass or drive the basketball.

Times had changed, and I needed to get a grip on what was going on in my life. More importantly, I could not believe that Janet did not have the courage to tell me and allowed me to get blind-sided by an accidental argument. I wondered if Janet would have told me if her sister had not blurted out the information. Wounded, I exited the parkway and eventually pulled into the driveway of my mom's house. Walking into the house my mom could tell something was wrong. Moms can always tell when something is up. My mom looking to stop me said, "Ken, you look like you got a monkey on your back. What's cooking?"

Here, my mom had given me a golden opportunity to get the monkey off my back, in her terms, and reveal that my baby had been aborted. Well that conversation was not going to happen as I would have to reveal too much information to my probing mom about my relationship with Janet. Looking my mom in the eyes I said "I don't know mom. I just don't know."

I slowly walked up the stairs to my room and closed the door. I laid on my bed and stared at the ceiling. Months ago, I stared at the same ceiling and dreamt of better days and a professional basketball career. Now those dreams seemed trivial as I now knew life was bigger than just basketball. I just wish the choices in life were just as easy as the choices in basketball.

My abortion experience with Janet was more traumatic than my abortion experience with Beth. With Beth, there had been some loss of trust and the seemingly distant relationship seemed to give her the right to make a difficult decision on our behalf in her best interest. In the case of Janet's abortion, I felt seriously betrayed because we talked often and she had to have an opportunity to tell me at some point. Clearly, she didn't tell me and that hurt. The impact of Janet's abortion decision changed our relationship in a more serious manner. We were not just boyfriend and girlfriend anymore. This was the woman who had my baby. As we went into my senior year, I started to focus on basketball again, and I mostly forgot about the abortion debacle.

As I laid in the bed, sick from my illness, I heard the beating heartbeat in my ear. It sounded like, *"ba bump, ba bump,"* and it got louder and stronger as I tried to quiet it. Was I responsible for the murder of my son from Janet? I did not make the call nor was I given any access. This did not give me any solace and more importantly I felt as if I was being punished by not being granted a son by God. How could such a horrible thing occur? My illness let me pick apart my actions in this crime and have pity for myself and the child. Ironically, I didn't feel that much pity for Janet as she allowed her parents to bully her and make the decision to kill our child without telling me. Distantly, in my mind, I felt that I wanted this baby. The life term punishment of not knowing what could have been haunted me, and I jockeyed with my past techniques to make this memory fade away.

13

THE FAIRFIELD YEARS

MY EARLY YEARS AT FAIRFIELD University were spent like a fish out of water. I gasped at air constantly as I was awkwardly in small talk conversation on topics that I knew relatively little about. I had not traveled to Europe in my high school years, and I almost knew nothing about sailing or yachting. On the other hand, I was well schooled on the best players in the National Basketball Association (NBA) like Julius Erving or John Havlicek. My world centered around sports, girls and cars.

During the late 70s, Fairfield University was, and still is, a top-notch educational experience that believed in educating the mind, soul, and spirit of the human being. Fairfield University had a full mandatory curriculum in the Arts which was just as rigorous as the math department. I knew many students who struggled learning about the meaning of Corinthian columns in Arts classes and could not pass the extremely difficult Art class exams. Fairfield University valued the broadening effect of the Arts and Religion on its students as these classes stretched my inquiry on the meaning of life in new and fascinating directions. After my Arts education from Fairfield University I never looked at big city architecture like New York or Chicago the same again. The big city was no longer asphalt and skyscrapers of concrete but a living organism that was trying to educate and talk back.

Ironically, the Fairfield University classroom experience gave me a platform to calm the cultural shock I experienced with my White classmates. I bonded with my White classmates on a level playing field where I could run with a conversation on English or pass them an idea to ponder with me. Although I was still a cultural fish out of water, Fairfield University provided me with oxygen and open water to roam the sea of opportunity without the bounds of any man's domain. I am sure I was exposed to racism with my White classmates at Fairfield University. I would remember the nasty small talk comments about inner cities or Black ghettos. But the real racism came as I was attracted to the beautiful White girls on campus but received the same negative experience my son received in White Richmond, Virginia. I never dated interracially at Fairfield University but attended the primarily White participant parties at the Stagger Inn or down by Jennings Beach. The White female dating experience escaped me at Fairfield University but it wasn't from a lack of trying. I vividly remember this beautiful brunette at one beach party, and we talked all night long. We were attracted to each other and I was ready to make a move on her to bring her home or back to my room. She knew my intentions and intercepted my move by saying, "You know I have never been with a Black guy." She continued, "You seem like a really nice guy and I like you but if my father knew I talked to or had a relationship with a Black guy he would kill me."

After hearing these words, I lost my appetite to have sex with the gorgeous brunette. This kind of experience was the norm for Black men on the Fairfield University campus as open interracial dating was not commonly accepted in the early 1980s.

I know my White classmates at Fairfield University would cringe if they knew they could be categorized at the same level of racism as the Capital of the Confederacy. Many Fairfield University students had a White Anglo Saxons Protestant (WASP) background and perceived their heritage superior or anti-racist when compared to Southern White supremacy. They would claim that they welcomed all races and did not hold Black men, women and children in chains and subject them to Jim Crow laws of bondage. But they did embrace economic disparities that set them above the norm while supporting educational institutions that held Black children at distinct competitive disadvantages. This ensured the probable success of White children at the expense of Black children which allowed a larger piece of the economic pie to flow to White communities from this pattern of disparate treatment and no one seemed to care. Fairfield University exposed these raw truths in the classroom and the priest urged its constituents to love and help their fellow man in life's cruel fates. Unfortunately, the real White world only embraced these messages at a superficial level and a glacier snail's pace of change. It was not until 2020 and the *Black Lives Matter* movement that you saw significant White participation in meaningful Black causes. My generation of White cohorts used racism to their advantage and embraced White privilege like a cold drink on a hot summer day. Fairfield University became the stage for many facets of my life to playout in a manner I could understand, accept and try to change for the better with the proper insight of an educated man.

One of the main characters and best teachers of life at Fairfield University was Fred Barakat, the head basketball coach at the university. Coach Barakat was a fiery Armenian from Union City, New Jersey who was a pretty good basketball player in the mold of Bob Cousy during his playing career. Coach Barakat and several good coaches like Jim Calhoun, Mike Krzyzewski, Dave Gavitt, Tom Penders, Rick Pitino and Dom Paterno battled each other relentlessly with passion, sweat, and guts for position in New England and Metro City basketball. Many of these coaches would go on to have Hall of Fame careers at larger universities willing to upgrade their basketball budgets unlike Fairfield University.

The East Coast Atlantic Conference (ECAC) was formed prior to the Big East basketball league and it was essentially a wild west of good basketball. Every college basketball team competed for a marketing or revenue advantage in the crowded corridor of New England and New York basketball. Fairfield University was a small university compared to the powerhouses like the University of Connecticut and Boston College, which had larger budgets and greater ambition which transpired into the Big East basketball conference formed by Dave Gavitt at Providence College.

Although Fred Barakat was hampered by the small budget attitude of Fairfield University his ambition and his drive was as large or larger than any rival that stepped in his path. Coach Barakat was a warrior and expected warrior mentality from his players on the court and off the court. Growing up in a tough Union City formed Coach Barakat into a fighter and he molded his players in his image to fight the giants of East Coast basketball dominance tooth and nail with pretty good success. Fairfield University basketball was known as Stagmania in its 1980s heydays and the games were always sold out and the style of play was electrifying. Coach Barakat employed tough defense with a running playground style to rack up many wins against good teams.

Fred Barakat was a winner and I wanted to win with him and for him. Most of the guys on the Fairfield basketball team looked up to Coach Barakat as a father figure and mentor over their college careers. I accepted the discipline that Coach Barakat enforced upon me as I entered Fairfield University as a freshman. I was a good basketball player, but my game needed work to get significant playing time. I understood Coach Barakat's thinking because although I was not a project, I was not a clear star at the division one basketball level. Coach Barakat did not make any promises about my playing time but I was guaranteed that if I worked hard that I would get on the floor and play. In my recruiting class Coach Barakat recruited myself, Hank Foster from Plainfield, New Jersey and Rich Diantonio from Lynbrook, Long Island. Hank was probably the jewel of the recruiting class as a talented small forward who could shoot and score although undersized. Rich Diantonio had the better press clipping as a star player on Long Island, New York. In retrospect I was probably the third leg of the recruiting class even though I committed to Fairfield University early in my senior year.

My freshman year at Fairfield University we had a stacked squad with Joe Deasantis and Flip Williams in the backcourt. Mark Young was a talented center who could shoot and got drafted by the Los Angeles Lakers. The rest of the squad was role players such as Mike Palazzi, whose father Togo was a former Boston Celtic and Rich Broginni a hard nose point guard also from Long Island. The only other Black guy who got playing time was Joe "Rock" Nelson, a talented forward from the Bronx, New York. Joe Rock was an interesting guy because he was probably the smartest guy on the team with the best body that drove the women crazy! We had a cast of confident characters and we went at each other hard in practice to settle who was going to play. Clearly Joey Desantis was the star and you had to make sure you did not hurt Joe D in practice or Coach Barakat would kill you. He treated Joe D like an only son as Joe would go on to have an excellent season and be drafted by the Washington Bullets. Flip Williams was a hard-nosed competitor and Coach Barakat's second son. He also could do no wrong although he had major deficiencies in his game such as dribbling. He was at best an undersized small forward trying to adjust to the second guard position. All other positions were up for grabs and in practice I went after Rich Broginni and Rich Diantonio. Clearly, I outplayed them but it didn't seem to matter to the coaches. I was not a pure point guard, but I could get the job done and thought I should get a chance to play. Our first game was on the road against the University of North Texas in a tournament sponsored by Tim Floyd and the University of New Orleans. We barely won as the scrappy Black team from Texas fought us tooth and nail. I clearly remember the game as Hank Foster got significant minutes and played well. Rich Broggini was the first guard off the bench and Rich Diantonio got significant minutes. I sat the whole game and did not play a minute. I was demoralized and my confidence fell to an all-time low. How could I outplay Broggini and Diantioni in camp and be denied a chance like everyone else? This was the politics of college basketball and many good players are told convincing stories to get them to commit to a university and then the coach has them captured. Coach Barakat could not even look at me after the game and assistant Coach Brendan Suhr acted like I did not exist. They knew I was pissed. They knew my emotional make up and I had just been punched in the gut. I floundered the first half of my freshman season as I would practice well and not play. Did Coach Barakat have something against me? Did I do something wrong? I was in the grip of Coach Barakat's psychological wheelhouse now and I was about to be taught some tough lessons about mental toughness.

   I was not the only player in the grasp of Coach Barakat's mental toughness school. Joe Nelson, the smart talented player from the Bronx, was also being mentally challenged by the coach. Joe did not make it through the season as he told Coach Barakat to kiss his Black ass after a grueling practice of Coach Barakat only screaming at Joe Rock. After Joe Nelson left, I was squarely in the eye of Coach Barakat. Coach Barakat needed players to step up out of their norm and play at a high level to support Joe Desantis and Mark Young. He did not need a player who would freelance or play outside the system. In my freshman year you could have nicknamed me "Ken outside the system Daniels ". Every time I saw an opportunity to score or make a play, I took it. This drove Coach Barakat nuts because I was supposed to get the ball to Joe Desantis to score or Mark Young. This was against everything I had been taught at the high school and playground level. I was like a wild horse that needed to be broken and Coach Barakat was the perfect overseer to break me in. It first started in practice that I got the demeaning barks of the head coach as he would fume at the mouth like a mad dog. After a simple play where I was supposed to pass and then pick for Joe Desantis the spirited coach yelled, "God dammit it Daniels! I told you to jump stop on the pick for Desantis and not run right into the man."

Once Fred Barakat picked you out for a small mistake, he would lean in to see if you could handle it. "Time out," yelled Coach Barakat.

In front of the whole team, Coach Barakat sought to light a fire in my ass. He said, "Daniels, what is wrong with you? Do you listen to what I say? Do you want to play?" Now was not a time to answer the angry Coach. He wanted to know that I was alive, that I had heart, that I was ready to sacrifice to get better his way and not my way. Not answering the Coach but staring right back at him I showed no emotion, no fear, and no tears. It was like I was back at home being forced to conform to the devious acts of my family members only I was willing to take the abuse to rise in the basketball world. I became a tough son of a bitch playing for Fred Barakat. Over the course of my freshman season, I rose from bench warmer to reserve point guard beating out the more experienced Rich Broggini and the more heralded Rich Diantonio. I welcomed the tough lessons from Coach Barakat unlike Joe Nelson. Which way was the right way? Leave the program like Joe Nelson or conform and compete like I did. Well Joe Nelson turned his ability to speak several languages and his debonair attitude into a topflight accounting job with the FDIC, which is not bad for a kid from the Bronx. In addition, Joe Rock kept his dignity as a proud Black man. He was too proud to ever be invisible. I admired the decision made by Joe, but I took a different avenue and conformed to the Fairfield way. I became invisible at times and accepted the White culture. At the time, its perks and benefits seemed to outweigh the cost of invisibility. To this day, I still do not know the cost of this type of existence nor does society.

My love for economics gave me a distraction from the demands for the game of basketball and the brutal mind games that seemed to follow basketball. I can remember the first time I read an economics book over the summer of 1979. I had a summer job as a janitor at Fairfield University arranged by the coaching staff. It seemed as if the White boys on the team got the nice office jobs in New York City for the summer, and I got some manual toiling janitors' job with a broom. I remember the broom just as much as the economics book because I would use both to balance my body as I read. Anchoring the broom on my left side and the economics book outstretched on my right side, I had a comfortable reading position. Boy did I love reading about the inner workings of capitalism and why it was justified to work so well through a complicated rationing system. I rarely used that broom in the summer of 1979. I guess the coaches knew it was an easy job, and I took the easy time to develop my academic mind along with my basketball game at the Pearl Street Summer League in Waterbury, Connecticut. I averaged thirty points on a run and gun team with my teammate-to-be Spencer Harrison, an all-state player from Holy Cross High School in Waterbury, Connecticut. Coach Barakat recognized my hard work over the summer and complimented me on my dedication. More importantly, he seemed committed to getting me relevant playing time, and I was pleased with my progress at Fairfield University on and off the basketball court.

Starting my sophomore year in the Fall of 1979, I was eager to resume my studies. I was ready to declare a major and economics seemed to fit me the best, but I wanted to first meet my professors. As I sat in the front row of the microeconomics class, I was surrounded by a sea of White faces with only Johnna Warner, the Black girl basketball player to break the White uniformity. Then a tall jolly guy walked in the room and he said, "I am Edward Deak. This is microeconomics, the most fascinating class you will ever take at Fairfield University."

This was my introduction to Dr. Deak who was a confident orator with an old school hair doo like Fonzy from *Happy Days*. Deak was just as cool as Fonzy as he had total command of the economics material. He mesmerized our classes with intriguing stories and direct questions to every student that had to be answered to demonstrate your adequate participation. I was hooked on Professor Deak as we developed a deep bond and friendship.

My relationship with Professor Deak was calm and nurturing which seemed to contrast the violent lectures I received from Coach Barakat. I think both men saw potential in me but used different methods to engage me. I preferred the cerebral, jovial approach of Dr. Deak. He prodded me along the way in economics projects with little seeds I could pick up along the way almost like feeding a baby chicken. There were no threats, no embarrassing moments, just a cool calm steady diet of intellectual food and boy was I hungry.

Contrary to my basketball experience, I flourished in the economics classroom and became known as the top economics student. I even won the economics essay contest and beat out Valerie Johnson Jarvis who was attending Fairfield University on a full academic scholarship. I attribute most of my success to the teaching style of Dr. Deak. I was a quick learner and adjusted my work ethic to the Fairfield atmosphere accordingly. Professor Deak noticed my drive and just put me in gear which contrasted with Coach Barakat who held me back to test my will. Eventually I would pass Coach Barakat's test, but I always wonder how far I could have gone in basketball if I received the right coaching that embraced my potential. I never got the chance to find out as Coach Barakat was fired at the end of my junior year. I lost my love for basketball between my sophomore and junior years due to the hostile learning environment. Fortunately, I found another love in economics and a nurturing teacher who opened the door to a feeding frenzy of knowledge and growth. Luckily for me one love left my heart and the new love for economics replaced the old love and more. In some respect that initial summer of 1979 with the broom allowed me to sweep the torturing means of control away from my mind and let peaceful knowledge replace the harsh words of wisdom. I never picked up a broom for work in my life ever again. I was on my way with the love of my life, economics.

Hanging in Bridgeport supplemented the lack of Black culture at Fairfield University. At Fairfield University, the Black student population was so low that all the Black students ate at one table during the meals in the cafeteria. Although the food was terrible the cafeteria provided a can't-miss social time as it was the time to catch up with everyone who was Black on campus. My closest Black friend on campus was Vinnie Jarvis, an engineering major from Bridgeport, Connecticut. Vinnie was a smart guy, but he was quiet and socially awkward. Everyone liked Vinnie because he did not have a bad bone in his body and was extremely helpful to everyone because he grew up in Bridgeport and the surrounding area. If anyone had questions about the area Vinny was the go-to-guy. Vinny and I would meet up at the cafeteria daily and Vinny would socialize with the White students more given he knew some from the local high schools. I on the other hand came from an overwhelmingly Black populated high school and town that had almost zero social interaction with White people. I found it strange that the Black students allowed themselves to be segregated at meal time at Fairfield University. The segregated meals symbolized all the evils of racism and the invisibility of the Black students to their White counterparts. For the White students, the Black students were not physically there because they did not try to interact with the Black students in any truly meaningful way. The Black students eating at their singular table reinforced the power structure of White society to the White students in a neat and tidy snack. To me the bizarre voluntary segregated cafeteria structure represented how White society's power structure had ring fenced the Black population all around the country so that they could redline services such as banking, education, healthcare and even food. These dynamics were strangling the Black community of much needed economic oxygen and the city of Bridgeport was a perfect example.

Vinny and I ventured off into Bridgeport often and visited with his brothers and family. Bridgeport in the early 1980s was at best a stagnant city and probably more accurately a city on the decline. The city had lost most of its industrial base and White flight to suburbs to towns like Trumbull, Darien and Chesire. This was a common trend, and this left Bridgeport with an inner-city core of primarily lower middle-class Blacks along with a growing population of struggling Puerto Rican immigrants. As I frequently visited with Vinny, I was struck by how severe the poverty was in Bridgeport and felt out of place as I was used to the pristine tree lined streets of East Orange. As a young man I was confused by the contrasting experiences of Bridgeport relative to East Orange. Although East Orange was a predominantly Black town it was a vibrant middle-class town with prideful people and employment was ample in the neighboring cities of New York, Newark and Jersey City. In addition, East Orange had a burgeoning Black professional middle class which represented the transition of Black Americans into mainstream America. Bridgeport on the other hand had a depressing local feel that centered on the declining smokestack factory economy. I can remember asking Vinny could we go fish in the Housatonic River which was close to his Bridgeport house. He replied, "You don't want to do that."

Looking at Vinny I found his answer strange. I said, "Why not?"

Chuckling, Vinny said, "Most of the fish are diseased from the pollution and you can't eat the fish."

The Housatonic River is a sprawling river that snakes its way through western Connecticut to the Long Island Sound. The polluted river symbolized to me the soul of the people of Bridgeport. Like the soul of Bridgeport and its people, the river was always flowing and useful. However, everything the river produced was dead and no one wanted to be bothered with it. This was the plight of many predominantly Black cities in America in the 1980s. White Americans just did not want to be bothered with the opportunity or the problems confronting Black Americans.

Although Bridgeport's economic picture was not that great the people had energy, grit and spunk. It was a fun city, although dangerous, and it had great parks to hang out in with plenty of fine young Black girls. Given the lack of Black girl population at Fairfield University, the Bridgeport girls provided an ample supply as did the Black girls at the University of

Bridgeport. Vinny and I got to know each other well during our off-campus transgressions. Vinny would go on to become a fine engineer and marry his Fairfield University sweetheart Valerie. Yes, the same Valerie that I beat in the economic essay contest. They would have a fruitful marriage with two girls. Unfortunately, Vinny died early from stomach cancer. I was not able to attend his funeral due to some work constraints. I wondered if Vinny's proximity to the Housatonic River and its toxins aided the cancer in his body. Bridgeport had potential but many good Black souls died in its toxic environment of discrimination and segregation.

Janet and I dated consistently from my sophomore year at Fairfield University until we were married in 1985. Looking back, I had no idea that she would eventually become my wife of 30 years. Small signs of her personality at Fairfield University should have been flags of concern for me but I ignored them as I was in love. For example, Janet was very shy, reserved, and was very matter of fact about a lot of life issues. Maybe this was your typical engineering attitude of indifference to creativity or passion, but I recognized it and I ignored it. Although we grew together as a couple, we probably should have been closer given the amount and quality of time we spent together. I was inseparable from Janet at Fairfield. She was my partner but was she my soul and life mate? Well we know the answer now but how did I miss the signs? Several signs were available, but I learned of them too late. I guess deep in my heart I knew that Janet was not my soulmate. I did not love Janet, or I should say I did not feel love for her. Of course, I loved her, but I was making a calculated decision at picking a partner that could help me succeed. Almost like picking a business partner that could sure up my weaknesses plus bring their skills to the table. If I am honest, I was being shrewd and a user of my wife to be a benefit to the both of us. I think my mother knew that I did not love Janet as she never voiced a positive opinion of her. I think moms always know when something is up, my father was excited as always for me and joked about Janet and I having children at some point. Other signs that I clearly knew of but underestimated their impact was the relationship with Janet's father. Mr. Norman was of Caribbean descent and clearly did not like Black people or he did not want a Black man marrying his daughter. How did I know that Mr. Norman was prejudiced against Blacks? Well, every time I visited South Jersey, he had a negative comment about Blacks in North Jersey and then one Thanksgiving I was clearly given a signal by the whole male side of the family when they chastised me as a nigger from North Jersey for the entire Thanksgiving dinner. I was so hurt and expected Janet to step in and defend me.

I remember saying to Janet, "Aren't you going to say something to your cousins."

Looking at me almost agreeing with them she said, "Well you are from East Orange and most South Jersey girls are afraid to date guys from the North."

I was just enlightened about the prejudice amongst Blacks and the prejudice between Blacks in South Jersey and North Jersey. In retrospect I should have known better and not been so naive. I should have known that I was marrying into Janet's family and that she could not just disown their existence if she wanted to remain in good standing with them. These factors manifested their ugly head at some point during our union and caused the foundation to crumble.

Bobby Hurt was my friend and basketball teammate at Fairfield University. We came from the same area of Essex County, New Jersey and hung out often after I graduated from Fairfield University. Bob was a close friend and we drank beer often together to have fun. Well one day we got drunk together and Bob said, "Hey, Ken, I got something on my mind I need to tell you."

I did not really know what Bob had on his mind as he was a constant jokester and liked to play pranks on people. I said, "Go ahead Bob. Tell me what's on your mind."

Suddenly Bob got serious and began to tell me a story that involved Janet. Bob said, "KD, you know you my boy, so I got to let you know."

Bob began to tell me a story that involved Janet and Barry, our Fairfield University classmate. Bob said, "Well KD, you remember when we would go on the road for our basketball games we would be away for a long time?"

Getting absorbed in the beer and Bob's story, I said, "Yeah."

Bob continued, "Well while we were away playing games, Barry was fucking Janet."

As soon as Bob said fucking, I almost pissed in my pants. You must remember, I was about 25 years into my marriage, and I was learning of the infidelity of my wife for the first time, if true. Bob's story made sense, and he really had no reason to lie. Gathering my senses, I asked Bob, "So Barry was fucking Janet while we were gone?"

Not speaking, Bob nodded his head yes. Naturally, I asked Bob, "How many times?"

Burping his beer, Bob slipped out, "Often."

I sunk into my chair with the new information and began to boil with anger. Sweet, innocent Janet was a cheat and a sneak. In fact, Janet turned out to be a good sneak and I never knew. I was totally blindsided but what should I do with the information? I confronted Janet with the information one day at home and she was speechless. She just did not have an answer. We did not speak for a couple of days and then we just moved on. Bob died unexpectedly in his sleep one night. I missed my friend terribly, but I am always grateful that he divulged what was on his conscience before he left. All I can say is, "Thank you Bob."

Janet's infidelity was the first sign of importance I missed. The second sign I missed involved our daily house duties in Ashland, Virginia, but it really started at Fairfield University. As Jan and I dated during our Fairfield days, we noticed that we had a lot in common. We both were good students and got along well with people. Our ambition was equivalent although Janet was a beast at organization and execution. She was a good match for me as I was a big thinker with good ideas but terrible at small details. Janet on the other hand was detail oriented to a fault and she was excellent at technical task and math. We bonded over long walks around Fairfield University's campus and seemed to have everything a young couple needed to succeed. However, we came from very different types of families. I came from a very traditional Baptist family that was warm and openly showed emotion and feelings. Janet came from an Episcopal family that was very reserved and rarely showed outward emotions toward each other. Her parents were extremely bright and were Master gardeners. I remember this because I was very interested in garden design and landscaping. Janet would brag about how her parents had these great gardens and how she planted all kinds of plants. I thought to myself, "Wow! Janet is perfect for me."

She gardens, cooks and is a hard worker ". As Janet and I started to live together after college I started to question our compatibility. Our initial home and our first purchase were in East Haven, Connecticut, where we purchased a two-bedroom condo for $25,000. It was a nice condo, but it had no gardens to my dismay and we jokingly called the condo, *Parking Lot*. The nickname was appropriate because you could almost drive up to the front door in the parking lot. Although the condo was not equipped with many amenities it was a great location to the City of New Haven with decent schools. As the Connecticut economy boomed, *Parking Lot*, the condo skyrocketed in price to $75,000. The Connecticut economy was in the midst of a housing bubble, and we would experience the downside of the bubble in the 1990s. However, it was the mid-1980s and we were growing as a couple and as professionals. Eventually, we had a home with extensive gardens all planted by me. Guess what? Janet hated gardening even though she came from parents who were Master gardeners. On our 10-acre lot I had a garden in almost every area. I had sun gardens, shade gardens, succulent gardens, rose gardens, etc. etc. I was a gardening fool. I loved it, and I wanted to share it with my wife. So, one day I made a point to get Janet in the garden. I went to Lowes, a local garden chain, and bought her some flowers for her own garden. Walking in the house I proclaimed "Hey Janet! Baby look, I bought these flowers to start the Janet garden." Almost rolling her eyes at me, she said, "I don't want to plant any flowers. I did all that stuff with my mother and father back in Belmar."

She then slipped back to her task after dismissing my agenda. I walked outside disappointed that Janet had no desire or inclination to spend any time with me outside. How could I incorrectly assess our compatibility on such a key issue. Over time, I planted thousands of bushes and plants at Quail Oak Court. It was my hope that I would grow old and just marvel over my years of work in the garden. Over 12 years of living at the Ashland house, Janet never planted one flower or bush and never came outside. Somewhere along the time of our marriage we had grown apart and the love we fostered at Fairfield University had vanquished. I had no direct evidence of this during my courting of Janet, but as our marriage developed, I would get clear signals or red flags that all was not well in our marriage garden.

My junior and senior year at Fairfield University were good years for me academically and athletically on the basketball court. I had worked hard in the summers on the basketball court and I had taken a scrawny 6'2" 175-pound frame and turned it into a chiseled 6'3" 198-pound frame with all muscle and low body fat. I had matured as a man and I had muscles upon muscles. Although I did not lift weights, I did all kinds of kinetic exercises which were very effective. My role with the team escalated as I was named team captain as a senior and earned the starting point guard spot as a junior. My work ethic carried above the battles with Rich Diantonio although he was clearly favored by Coach Barakat. I remember our first tournament of the year at the Clemson IPTAY Classic and we upset Rice in the first game with Ricky Pierce, the future NBA All-Star and Milwaukee Buck.

In the second game, we faced Clemson and Larry Nance. Larry Nance was a high flying forward and future NBA first round pick. In that game, we gave Clemson all they could handle but lost by about five points. I made the all-tournament team, along with Nance and Pierce, by scoring 29 points against Clemson as I destroyed their backcourt. It was probably the best game of my career and demonstrated my work and skill level was at an acceptable Division 1 level. After the game, I expected some recognition from Coach Barakat but got no signal of approval or emotion. He was pissed we lost the game and was more concerned with chewing out our star forward, Rich Wejnert, from Jersey City. I grinned to myself and patted myself on the back for my achievement and was glad that Coach Barakat had moved on to a new psychological victim. I finally had learned to deal with Coach Barakat and the mental pressure he created. These skills would be helpful in my future career and I never looked back.

Off the basketball court, my junior and senior year were rewarding but no without their own set of dilemmas. Probably the biggest challenge I had was to set my sights on a master's degree from the University of Connecticut but in the summer of 1981, I was selected to participate in the American Economic Association (AEA) summer program at Yale University. The program was a selective summer honors program aimed at increasing minority participation in the social sciences such as economics. I was nominated for the program by Dr. Deak and he encouraged me to apply for the summer program and to look at graduate degree programs at the same time. I was thrilled to have the support of Dr. Deak which felt awkward as I felt aided by his enthusiasm. He seemed to have more confidence in me than I had in myself. This was a stark contrast from my basketball experience. However, I had a real dilemma on my hands as we had just hired a new Coach, Terry O'Connor from Harvard University and I would have to battle all over again for my starting spot on the basketball team. If I were dedicated to my basketball game, I would skip the AEA summer program and go play in the New Haven and Waterbury summer leagues. I was well known in Connecticut and the team organizers were inquiring if I wanted to play. I needed some help in making this decision as it could have some long-term implications. Who could I turn to for such advice? My father knew a lot about education, but he had no clue about sports. I could not ask Coach Barakat as he was fired and on his way to the ACC. Janet was skilled in the details of organizations but did not have a grasp of the big picture. I finally arranged a meeting with Dr. Deak, and we had an in-depth conversation on my future. Dr. Deak was the right person to discuss my future as he was a sports advocate and he knew the academic landscape along with the job prospects in the area. I walked into Dr. Deak's office and he always said "Sit down Ken". This made me feel welcome and relieved me of any anxiety associated with my dilemma of basketball versus the AEA program. I began to explain my dilemma and Dr. Deak, fully understanding the choice, cut me off and said, "Ken you don't have a choice if you are smart."

    He said it with such conviction that I could not wait to hear his rationale. He went on to explain that, while I was a good basketball player, I had a real gift in the field of economics. He then went into the numbers to convince me that he was not making it up or promoting some emotional decision on his part.

    He said, "I have seen you play and you are a lot better than what they give you credit for, but at best there is probably a 1% chance that you could become a professional basketball player."

I did not say anything and I kinda stared down at the floor, but my ears were wide open. Dr. Deak continued in jest, "Heck, I'll even double it and say you have a 2% chance of making the NBA."

I got his point clearly. Relying on basketball only was a gamble and a high-risk gamble. Sensing my openness to his opinion Dr. Deak started to describe how wonderful the AEA summer program was and the doors it would open if I completed the honors economics program. He was right. I decided to concentrate on economics in the summer of 1981 and not play any summer league basketball for the first time in a very long time. Ironically, I did not miss basketball at all and met some wonderful people at Yale University, including Donald Brown, the world-famous economist. The result of my decision resulted in me being recruited by some of the best PhD economics programs in the country. In some ways it was ironic that a Black kid's denial of the traditional Black city game turned him into a highly recruited academic scholar in the traditional White Ivory Tower. America was trying to change and transform into a more perfect union and programs like the AEA summer program saw the gap in qualified minority applicants and applied a solution. I benefited greatly from my academic experience at Yale University. I clearly was not the top economics student in the honors summer program, but I came back to Fairfield University with super confidence in my economics background. I demonstrated those skills weekly in my economics classes and most of the White students came to me for the more difficult answers with certain economic questions. I had seen the material before at Yale and I was just repeating what I had learned. It came easily and naturally just like a foul shot. Fairfield University recognized my achievement as a student, and I was honored with an academic student achievement award with all the top students. I had again used my work ethic to rise to the top of the field but now I was left with one last dilemma involving Janet.

My final dilemma between myself and Janet during our final year at Fairfield University was our union after my graduation. I had gotten into several top economics graduate schools such as the University of Wisconsin and the University of Connecticut. Janet on the other hand was in a joint degree program between Fairfield University and the University of

Connecticut. She had completed three years at Fairfield with the core classes and was now headed to the University of Connecticut for the final two years of the engineering classes. Looking back, it seemed like a match made in heaven that Janet and I would head off to Storrs, Connecticut together to further our education. For me it was a tough choice as the University of Wisconsin was a better-quality choice as a Big Ten institution. However, attending the Big Ten university would probably end my relationship with Janet as the distance would be significant and clearly absence makes the heart wander. I chose the University of Connecticut to be close to Janet, as I was in love. I remember telling Dr. Deak, who was a University of Connecticut PhD alum, of my decision and he just shook his head without mentioning a word. His reaction implied I was giving up a significant opportunity. My decision to attend the PhD program at the University of Connecticut had a lot of personal benefits that going to Wisconsin would eliminate. First, I would stay on the East coast and maintain my family ties along with my close friends. I would also make some great friends at the University of Connecticut as I was familiar with the area. Second, I got a nice scholarship from the University of Connecticut and the American Economic Association which made my cost of attendance low. Finally, I was able to keep my bond with Janet strong and our love continued to grow even though it would be challenged by the large school party atmosphere of the Connecticut Huskies. Janet and I closed the final chapter on our Fairfield University association with a nice dinner at the Angus Steakhouse near the Merritt Parkway. I thought it was a nice way to celebrate our achievement for our hard work at the university and to celebrate our perseverance as a couple. Many couples who attended Fairfield University ended up as married couples as Fairfield University was a feeder school for WASP girls to meet the perfect gentleman appropriate for their family. Janet and I found each other based on our natural attraction for each and not by some ad hoc selection method based on class, economics and race. I really thought we had the ingredients for a lifetime of happiness together. We didn't make it to a lifetime, but we did have the time of our life while it lasted and I wouldn't change my path or our trajectory for any cultural promotion process.

14

THE UCONN YEARS

I ENTERED THE UNIVERSITY of Connecticut (UCONN) with mixed emotions after graduating from Fairfield University. First, I was a former rival of the Huskies basketball team and I would see the players around town like Cliff Robinson, a UCONN basketball star, during his tenure. They recognized me and curiously asked me what I was doing on campus. I did not really answer them as describing my academic ambition did not feel right at the time. I did not have any misconception that my best basketball days were behind me, but I did play in the intramural league. In the intramural league, I made some lifelong friends like Bill Brandon who turned out to be an outstanding Black professional in the insurance industry. Second, I also wasn't totally convinced that a master's degree would position me any better in the job market, but it was the best deal I had going for me. I didn't want to pursue an MBA and limit my field of study to just business, so my choice of economics was a risk. I had not decided to pursue a PhD in economics yet, and I was trying to figure out the dynamics of my future opportunities. Finally, Janet and I were still tied at the hip and our relationship would be tested by the many new relationships on the UCONN campus.

Back in 1979, UCONN was a diamond in the rough. The physical plant of the campus had gone through significant deterioration as the state of Connecticut had fallen upon hard times due to poor business conditions and the beginning of a housing bubble implosion. The campus reflected the strain of the state budget as it had not had any significant investment in years. The clad on the main library reflected this disinvestment as the exterior of the building was literally falling apart but was wrapped in a cascading net to capture the falling debris. Compared to Fairfield University's physical campus UCONN was a dump and the students were a whole lot grittier than the usual preppy guy that attended Fairfield University. More importantly for me, UCONN had a sizable Black and minority population which made the social circle much more interesting and dangerous for my relationship with Janet. Actually, as I started to get around campus, economics was the last thing on my mind as I was having too much fun. The four years of Fairfield University had left me deprived of any significant social interaction with any significant number of Black people. The initial days of UCONN were spent just meeting new people and talking. The Black guys were cool at UCONN as most were good students but also sought a social life. UCONN was the flagship university in the UCONN higher education system so most students were competitive and came from good schools. This made my transition easy as I was with like-minded students that had goals.

My living conditions were pretty good as I lived in the graduate dorms on campus which was almost right in the center of campus but near the library. Although UCONN's physical campus was in disrepair, the beauty of the campus was evident, and the layout of the school was much more efficient than Fairfield University. I guess when you have over 15,000 students that things need to move smoothly since the students need to interact and use the facilities with ease. My daily routine started with breakfast but the graduate dorms didn't have any cafeteria facilities, so I had to walk across the street to the nearest dorm cafeteria. This forced me into the UCONN undergraduate population, and I met all kinds of people at the cafeteria. This contrasted the isolated, solitary, all Black table of students at Fairfield University with the multicultural table of the students at UCONN. The difference was as striking as night and day as students of all races co-mingled interchangeably at UCONN. I also noticed that interracial dating was a more common occurrence at UCONN, and I met several Black guys that openly dated White girls. While the UCONN social scene was a freer environment among the races than Fairfield University, the White cultural dominance was also pretty obvious as the music at the bars still tended to be rock and roll rather than the silky rhythm and blues of the hip Black bands. Rock and roll were mixed with a high level of beer consumption such that on any weekend night UCONN transformed from the flagship educational institution into one of the better party schools in the nation. At first, I didn't embrace the party school activities at UCONN as I spent most of my weekend time with Janet, and we would either drive home to New Jersey to see family or visit old friends in Hartford or New Haven. Janet and I as a couple did not embrace the party activities at UCONN as Janet did not meld into the social activities in Storrs easily. In addition, her engineering requirements were so rigorous that she would study on weekends, often for her exams or just have study groups, for such topics as structural dynamics or introduction to civil engineering. I admired Janet's dedication to her craft, but it left me a lot of time to ponder my future and to explore the Storrs social scene. For the first time in my adult life, I was free to explore a multicultural social environment without any boundaries on my capabilities except my conscience to be faithful to my relationship with Janet. At UCONN, I wasn't an invisible Black man but an inquisitive social animal trying to figure out my place in the social fabric.

I eventually gave into the party animal antics of UCONN school life. Everyone was having a good time on the weekend except for Janet and her engineering cohort. I even had a Black colleague from the economics department that was a party animal. Frank was my buddy in the economics department studying international economics with an interest in international business. Frank was a Black student from Panama, who was a good student, but he was a social animal that attracted all kinds of people when it was time to have a good time. What boggled my mind was that Frank wasn't an overly attractive guy but he had an island suaveness that drove the legions of White girls mad at UCONN. I, on the other hand, still was not a party guy and I struggled to be an extrovert in the UCONN social scene. I do remember one encounter which summarizes my capabilities to take advantage of the UCONN social scene. Frank and I had studied very hard all week and had taken care of our economics department responsibilities. As the weekend approached, Frank always had a plan for the weekend parties and I usually just tagged along because it was going to be lively and full of beautiful women. I asked, "Hey Frank, where's the party this weekend?"

Frank chewing his gum in a cool fashion said, "The undergraduates are giving a big party at Hilltop dorm."

Frank always knew the information on the parties and where to go. Finishing his task and spitting his gum in the wastebasket, Frank looked at me and said, "Why don't you come on out and meet me there around 9 p.m."

Frank and I were like a team when we went out. I don't know why Frank wanted me around for the party antics because once we got there, he had the vibe going and the girls dancing. I am not sure Frank was sexually active with the legion of White girls that followed him. I think they admired his free-flowing island vibe and he became almost a campus cult icon of pure fun. Clearly Frank wasn't invisible but I am not sure that he was taken serious by his band of White friends. It all seemed like a silly game to me.

I met Frank at the Hilltop dorm at about 9:30 pm this chilly Storrs weekend and I remember the weather because I left my sweater in the graduate dorm room and I was pissed. It was cold outside as I drove over to the undergraduate dorm on the chilly Saturday evening. As I walked into the dorm, it was packed with the usual suspects of drunk White guys, soon to be drunk White girls along with loud rock and roll music. Frank had gotten there early and was in the middle of the hallway dancing with two White girls hanging all over him. Seeing me, Frank smile and nodded with his head as a signal that things were in place for a good time. I smiled back at Frank and took up station with a cup of free beer in my hand off to the side as I tapped my feet to the rock and roll music. As I stood for a while suddenly, I heard my name called, "Ken, is that you? Ken Daniels from Fairfield."

As I looked up, I saw this thickly built cute White girl smiling at me. At first, I didn't recognize her but then it started to come together. Kate was a local high school girl from Fairfield that always attended the Fairfield basketball games with her Black friend, whose name I never did know back at Fairfield. I knew Kate's face well as she would always smile at me during the pre-game warmups at Fairfield basketball games, and we had been introduced by a Fairfield alumnus one time. She was an energetic high school student back then and I never took her smiling face as more than an interested basketball fan back at Fairfield. Responding back, I said, "Kate, how are you? What are you doing here?"

Smiling back at me with a beer in her hand she said, "This is my dorm. What are you doing here?"

Kate was with a friend and she was clearly buzzed from the beer and slightly giggling at me. At this point, I was just enjoying the music and observing the party scene. As the night went on Kate got drunker and drunker and by the end of the night, she was sloppy drunk. I myself was drunk by this time as I drank by myself all night off to the side of the party watching Frank do his thing. Suddenly I felt a tap on my shoulder and immediately I smelled the beer. Slowly turning it was Kate smiling at me again and putting her arms up around my shoulder. She was leaning on me and swaying to the music as she said in a drunken manner, "You know at Fairfield I always had a crush on you."

I must admit at this time I sensed an opportunity but I was dizzy drunk, and I just smiled and grinned at Kate. Kate continued speaking, as she was clearly not all there, "Why don't you and me go to my room and have some drinks?"

I chuckled as Kate thought of drinking more as she clearly had enough beer. However, I was tired of the rock and roll music and it was getting late. Without saying a word Kate grabbed my hand and led me out the room and down the hall to her dorm room. All of a sudden, the loud rock and roll music turned into a quiet setting with Kate and I alone in her room. However, Kate was hell-bent on drinking more. She had more beer and liquor in her room and I was taken aback by the quantity of alcohol available. Shoving a beer in my face she said, "Drink," and I subtly drank because that's what you did at the UCONN party scene.

Kate and I drank a few more beers and we reminisced about old Fairfield as we sat on her bed. Finally, our conversation ran out of steam and

Kate kissed me. At first, I didn't know what to do as her tongue rammed down past my tongue and almost into my throat. I grabbed her back and kissed her just as forcefully. Kate was suddenly on top of me kissing and we were making out on the bottom of her bunk bed when I started to feel queasy as the odor of her beer filled my mouth and permeated my nose. Grinding on top of me she was in a trance and her breast pressed into my chest. At this time, I should have been focused on Kate's advancement but I couldn't get the powerful beer smell out of my mind or nose. The constant rocking motion and the overconsumption of beer came to a head for me and I gently pushed Kate to the side and ran out the room.

I still remember her bewildered face looking at me as I rushed out of the door and outside beside my car. I began to throw up violently as I was not a heavy drinker and the beer had done a number on my head and stomach. As I finished throwing up, the cold air quickly reminded me that it was not smart to be outside without a coat. I jumped in my car but I was in no condition to drive as the car spun without moving. I did not even start the car as the car insides initially pulled the cold air off my neck and back. Slowly I drifted off to sleep and images of Kate, Frank and the party floated through my head.

The night went by quickly and as morning came, the sunlight rose. I woke up in my car behind the Hilltop dorm in the parking lot. As I woke, I shivered as the cold reclaimed my body and I started my car. I quickly drove to the graduate student dorms where I got out of the car and ran to my dorm room. Still slightly sick with a hangover I started a hot shower and jumped in to get warm. The warm water felt good and relieved my aching body of the beer induced pain. As the warm steam from the water filled my nose with comfort, I began to cough and I vomited some more as the final beer poisoning left my body. Turning off the shower, I quickly dried off and fell on to my warm bed. I slept for hours and missed class the next day. The following day I saw Frank in the economics department and he said, "Where have you been? That chick that you were dancing with at the party was looking for you."

I assumed that Frank meant Kate and I felt bad about our experience. She was a nice girl and I failed at my hook up with the cute sexy Fairfield kitten. I felt embarrassed by the whole encounter and it was wildly different from my Fairfield University experience with the White girls. My embarrassment quickly faded to some strange animal pride as I had conquered a barrier of racial divide as an inner-city Black youth. I never saw Kate again but I did get a phone call from her when I was a professor at VCU some 30 years later. We laughed about the encounter and she was happily married with a child living in Massachusetts. Her son was looking at attending VCU and she ran across my profile doing her research on the university. Much had transpired in my life since that drunken night on the UCONN campus but somehow the past seemed to follow me. Little did I know at the time that you reap what you sow and although I was a graduate student at a fine New England university, I was not ready for the commitment. My behavior on that cold UCONN night reflected on my lack of focus on my academic studies. Soon I would try to refocus my commitment on my studies and my relationship with Janet but I was behind the eight ball as Janet was committed to her studies and faithful to our relationship. Boy did I have a lot to learn.

Early into my UCONN experience I had fallen into a lackadaisical trap that was content with just getting by. This violated my work ethic along with my tried and true pattern to always put my best foot forward. My UCONN economics professor saw my lack of commitment and sought to motivate me with a series of low grades on assignments such as a B and C+ on econometrics and economics history assignments, respectively. A C+ in graduate work was equivalent to a D in undergraduate work at best. I got the message quickly and attempted to improve my reputation and my study habits. I shifted my alliances in the economics department and started to talk more with Peter Velz, an astute student of history and facts, who always was straight-faced and on task. Peter was a nice guy who was kind of quiet but well-liked by all the economics students. He seemed to have figured out the economics department and had a natural affinity for all economics related topics. In short, he was a walking encyclopedia but he wasn't a nerd and knew how to have fun.

I needed to mimic more of Peter's characteristics if I wanted to improve as an economic major and become a serious student of my craft. It worked as my grades improved and I began to understand the subject and recognized where my strengths lied. I was more of a technician and technical expert in economics and less of a soft issue analyst and a purveyor of facts and figures like Peter. Manolis Paximadas was a Greek economics major and he had similar technical skills like me and we started to talk more about the subject and developed a bond. Frank continued his superficial commitment to the subject as he and I drifted apart. As I started to spend more time in the economics department, I started to learn that my study mates were not all work and no play. Peter, a White male, had started dating Orawin, a Taiwanese young lady who was sharp as a tack and Manolis was dating Asha, a short sexy Indian girl who was a friendly person to all. How did I miss the shenanigans of my economics cohorts? Life in the economics department became more interesting, fun, and challenging as we all attempted to find our way and fulfill our promise.

Peter went on to graduate and become a top CIA analyst at the highest level and have an outstanding government career. Orawin graduated with her PhD and worked for Fannie Mae, the government mortgage association. Manolis went on to become the Director of Actuarial Informatics at Aetna insurance in Hartford, Connecticut. I was not aware what happened to Asha, but I believe she and Manolis got married and had children. Clearly my cohort of UCONN graduates were successful and it would be nice for the department to honor its early graduates one day.

I never really bonded with any of the faculty in the economics department like I did with Dr. Deak at Fairfield University. There were several professors that I liked but most of the professors seemed aloof and always self-absorbed with their research agendas. Anytime you sat down with a professor to talk the conversation almost certainly shifted to their agenda and their viewpoint of some esoteric economic topic. I did not find any professor that attempted to motivate me or any of my classmates in any visible way. The department did have some clear favorites as certain students fit the stereotypical vision of the department's model student. I clearly was not built in this mode and I had already made up my mind to start a counter intuitive plan of study to break the outdated monotony of the UCONN economics department. This was a risky move but it was the right move at the right time and I benefited from my forward-thinking approach to the subject. As time moved on the economics curriculum got more rigorous and all masters' students were required to take a written exam on the entire field of economics in macroeconomics and microeconomics. The professors could ask you any questions on anything considered fair game on the application of the field or from the well-known literature in the field. Past exams were available to be reviewed and they show a tendency for the microeconomics questions to be an unknown application of the subject while the macroeconomics questions tended to be literature based. Studying for the master's exam was a Herculean effort that required the material to be mastered and memorized for certain economic time periods that mattered. I took the exam and it lasted for at least a three-hour period. The room was so quiet that you could walk on the thick tension in the air. Some students were visibly panicking during the exam, but I focused on my study habits and got the full exam done. I had put forth a good faith effort and I felt good about my preparation, execution, and performance.

I remember hearing that the results of the master's exam were available and every student had to go to their faculty advisor at the time to get their result. My advisor was William McEachern who was a classy good-looking established type of man who was one of the better undergraduate teachers at UCONN. He was sought out by undergraduate students for his thoughtfulness and ability to communicate. I was a teacher assistant for Professor McEachern as part of my scholarship. He treated me well and always with respect. I made an appointment to meet with him to discuss my master's level exam and he quickly obliged to the time. I remember walking into his office and he was smoking his pipe as usual and it had a soothing odor and it looked cool although I didn't smoke. Professor McEachern just looked and fit the part of a well-connected professor and it was known that he had a lot of connections to the state legislature in Hartford. Walking up to his door, he said, "Come on in Ken."

I cautiously approached and he said, "I know you want to know about your exam. You did well. You passed."

I breathed a sigh of relief as I had cleared a difficult hurdle that many of my classmates did not clear as I would learn later. The master's level exam was the most difficult process I ever went through and the exam forced me to dig deep into my studying process and creativity to provide a viable solution under pressure.

I said, "Thank you Professor McEachern."

Professor McEachern continued smoking on his pipe then he stopped and looked up from his chair and said, "Ken, you will do well as you leave UCONN. You are an authority figure and people will look up to you."

He then continued smoking his pipe as to dismiss me from his presence without saying goodbye. I smiled at Professor McEachern and without saying goodbye or thank you, I turned around and started walking down the economics hall proudly. I was now a master's graduate of the UCONN economics department. I dreamed of going to Wall Street and applying for the lucrative analyst jobs or maybe following in my father's footsteps in education. I didn't have a concrete plan, but I knew my chances of being successful had just gotten better with my higher level credentials. UCONN was good for me and helped me develop the aptitude to be a successful professional and the character to deal with all kinds of people fairly.

With the successful completion of my program, I looked for Janet to share the good news. I found her in her dorm room and she was looking out the window staring astutely. I walked in smiling and gave her a hug. She said, "Hey, how are you doing?"

I smiled and said, "Guess what?"

Looking at me and smiling she said, "You passed".

I replied, "You know it!"

Janet and I hugged each other and screamed in joy as we had completed the first leg of our dream together. She said, "We have to celebrate! What do you want to do?"

I did not have an answer for Janet as I was just basking in my accomplishment and enjoying the moment with her. I do not think Janet and I went anywhere that night. I did not have the money to celebrate and Janet was not a party person. We just ate in her room and talked about our future and the possibilities. Janet being Janet began to drill down on the actual plan and began to talk about her opportunities and how my degree would allow me to get a job near her. She began to explain that she was sending her resume out to engineering firms in New York, New Haven, and Hartford. I listened to Janet but I wasn't ready to connect the dots to the actual plan and the minutia of detail necessary to make the plan a reality. This would set a pattern in our relationship as Janet was always the effective executor of our plan. I was the set-up guy who drove the general direction. Janet, knowing my habits shook my arm and said, "Ken, are you listening to me?"

I nodded my head and affirmed I was getting the gist of what she was saying. Laying back on her bed I listened to Janet lay out her ideas and I began to think of my future with her and what I wanted with my newly found degree. Jan and I stayed connected through our UCONN excursion as a couple. We survived my indiscretions and stayed focused on the prize offered by our education. For young Black adults, education was a necessary requirement to keep up with the ever-increasing competitive job market. Our love also proved resilient in the face of challenges and that proved to be authentic for most of our married lives together. I had my life-partner to work through the ups and downs of starting a long arduous journey. We were ready to leave UCONN and start the journey.

Janet was my main support while I was at UCONN but my other "ride or die partner" was a friend I made while playing intramural basketball, Larry Hayden. Larry was an Eastern Connecticut High School basketball star that never made an attempt to further his education, as far as I knew, and had started an early family with his young daughter Denise. He had left the mother of his daughter but had to provide for his young daughter, so he got a job in the mailroom at the UCONN.

I would see Larry every now and then on campus. We would meet to play basketball at lunchtime in the UCONN fieldhouse. Larry was a very good basketball player and he was on the other team but I wasn't guarding him. He was an excellent shooter and he began to destroy this guy guarding him and pushed his team out to an early lead in the game. Not to be out done, I started playing hard and keeping our team in the game and eventually the game was tied at 20 to 20. I said, "Time out. I got him," referring to Larry.

I was not going to let Larry win this game and get knocked off the basketball court as it took a long time to get a run on the basketball court. They passed the ball back in and I denied Larry touching the ball but one of his teammates got an easy basket and his team won the game. Still closely standing next to each other Larry said, "You lucky I didn't get the ball. You know I would have busted you."

I said, "You must be dreaming."

We chuckled at each other and started a lifelong friendship that included playing on intramurals together as Larry asked me to join his team. I learned a lot about Larry and his family as he invited me often to his mother's house in Willimantic for dinner. Larry was originally from Mississippi and his family migrated to Willimantic to work in the vibrant thread mills that used to populate the city. His mother was adorable and Larry would call her Josephine and I called her Ms. Josephine. She would cook for us and make us laugh. She was the matriarch of Larry's family like Mama Dear of my family. Women like Mama Dear and Josephine knew how to pass wisdom down by tales and stories of their enduring faith in God. Many nights, she schooled Larry and me on the do's and don'ts of life. Larry became almost like a brother to me during my stay in Storrs and it pained me that I was likely going to leave him as I had finished my Master's program.

One weekend, Larry and I were sitting at Tony pizza having a beer and joking about our hang out escapades in Manchester and Hartford. Larry and I went out almost every weekend and I was there when he met his lifelong sweetheart, Darlene from Hartford. Larry had a big laugh and was the town jokester. His playful attitude made him a great guy to be around as he was a genuine soul and laidback. Larry and I were very different educationally but we were alike in many respects. We did the best with the cards that we had been dealt and did not step on people to advance our own situations. I felt bad that Larry never got the chance to finish college given his paternal situation. He was a smart guy and given the right situation, he would have thrived and advanced given his ability. However, he never complained and just kept on working, kept on providing, kept on believing that better days were ahead without any proof. As Josephine told us many times in her own words, "Don't worry Ken, God will provide."

I would never tell Josephine or Larry but I was reluctant to leave my destiny in the hands of a mythical God whom I believed in but never outwardly connected to in any manner. I would have a whole different tune about God after the challenges of my life, career, and sudden illness. I didn't know what the immediate future held for me but I knew it would be more fun and more secure if I had my buddy Larry to look out for me. After I left UCONN I never found a friend that I could trust without fear ever again.

15

IVORY TOWER

I GRADUATED FROM THE PHD economics program at the University of Connecticut in 1990 with a specialization in finance. My dissertation was a finance dissertation that applied the Kalman Filter, a digital signal processing technique, to the term structure of interest rates and dividend signaling policy. The Kalman Filter is a legendary smoothing technique that was invented primarily in rocket technology to ensure that rockets hit their target. Today it is applied in many fields such as electronics, finance and machine learning such as artificial intelligence. I remember defending my doctoral thesis to the economics department and my thesis received a lukewarm reception by my audience because they did not quite understand the importance or use of the Kalman Filter. However, my faculty advisors on my dissertation understood the amount of work I put in to teach myself a technique not taught in the economics department and approved my PhD in economics.

My core curriculum was unique and much different than any other economics students in the program. I took most of the finance core classes and specialized in different electives offered by the university such as digital signal processing. In 1988, I applied the Kalman Filter to economics and finance problems which was an advanced track of study and against the grain or counter intuitive to the traditional methods accepted in the marketplace of ideas. I was unique in my program of study and I was unique as a Black man in 1988 competing against some of the best finance minds in the country. Not only was I the only Black PhD in the economics program but I was the only Black PhD interviewing on the job market at the major finance conferences such as the Financial Management Association and the Eastern Finance Association. I was like a unicorn as a species and I was trying to compete in a White male dominated field of higher education appropriately known as the "Ivory Tower".

To be quite honest Fairfield University prepared me well for my unique experience of being the only Black male in rigorous classes. At Fairfield University, I took the core math classes but also the same math classes as the math majors such as Logic. Ironically, the class on Logic had no numbers and I remember the math majors at Fairfield University looking at me like I was a ghost. They often said are not you Kenny Daniels on the basketball team. I would politely answer, "Yes."

Then I knew the next question would be interesting. One student asked, "Why would you take this hard math class instead of some easy sociology class or psychology."

At that time, I really didn't have a good answer and usually just blurted out, "I like math; it's fun."

What I really wanted to say was, "Why wouldn't I take the best available classes to give myself the best opportunity to compete and win against people like you? Why would I take easy classes and not do my best?"

Later in my life I would pass these simple messages of aspiration on to my children, and they also aspired to do more rather than less.

This line of questioning and doubting continued at the University of Connecticut. You must remember, I was a Black male in the mid-1980s studying theoretical finance for financial research at the highest level of competition. We were not being trained for secondary education or even Wall Street. I was being trained to solve the world's financial problems or at least contribute to understanding them better.

One of the key classes in the finance curriculum was the theoretical corporate finance class. It was a keystone course which usually determined the ability of a finance student. The best students in theoretical corporate finance can get the top jobs as asset pricing specialist or entry level professorships at the top universities. I always sat in the front of the class to make a statement that I was a serious student. On the first day of the theoretical corporate finance class the professor walked in the class and welcomed all the students then he looked at me. Looking straight in my face he said " Young man are you sure you are in the right class ". Always expecting the unusual or unknown from my teachers when I started a semester, I smiled at him and said, "Yes sir."

I will admit, I was taken aback by his stance and the other students thought they were more talented than I as a given. I immediately transported to my father's rants in my mind about White boys kicking my ass implying they would out achieve or out compete me. Now I was finally understanding the madness of my father's message and its source of empowerment to compete with vigor and honor as a badge of courage. As a Black man, I was to fight the good fight even when the odds are stacked against you to advance the cause of "enlightenment". Enlightenment was a burden where I always had to prove myself to my doubters, my antagonist, and the racists in the Ivory Tower. Yes, the Ivory Tower not only houses racism, but it promotes it directly and indirectly by its selection process of students and hiring of certain professors based on an ad hoc committee selection process.

As I was interviewing for jobs after my University of Connecticut graduation, which I didn't bother to attend, I relied heavily on my professors and their connections to get a proper placement in the job market. I did not attend the graduation for my PhD because I did not seek the approval of the economics faculty or the university faculty as a meaningful goal. I knew I was invisible to most of the faculty and only a few faculty members had good intentions of helping Black PhD students such as myself. In hindsight, I wish I had attended the graduation as my attendance may have provoked the imagination of one Black kid in the stands or enlightened the mostly White graduation audience that there was a Black PhD in economics from Connecticut about to enter a hostile world for Black professionals. One faculty who looked out for me was my advisor, Carmelo Giacotto, and he supported me through my dissertation process so that I finished and I got a job. Carmelo was a talented Italian finance professor who had navigated the roadblocks of academia and maintained his sense of humor and balance. He was a cool professor that made work fun but he was a little quirky and invited us to his house for a cookout in the freezing cold. We cooked out in the freezing weather and Carmelo smoked a little pot. I thought this was odd for a university professor, but it showed his humanity. I thank Fairfield University all the time for requiring me to think broadly about all situations. Francis Ahking was also instrumental in my success as my dissertation advisor in the economics department. Francis was almost the opposite of Carmelo. Francis was a strict professor and he was almost always serious and probably uptight. Francis was an Asian professor who got his PhD from Virginia Tech University. In hindsight, I think Francis felt some of the evils of the Ivory Tower and handled them as best he could. I had a lot of respect for Francis as he kept his word to help me finish my dissertation despite all my imperfections and weaknesses.

Many PhDs never finish their academic programs or get proper placement in the job market after graduation. Carmelo let Neil Murphy, a professor at Virginia Commonwealth University (VCU), know about my potential and my character. This informal vouching system is critical in the higher education placement process and not well known or understood by inexperienced university administrators or by university administrators who come from the private sector with no knowledge of the intricate working of the research mission or function.

I had met Neil Murphy before I started my PhD program as a bank analyst at the Bank of New England in Springfield, Massachusetts in the mid-1980s. Neil was a heavy weight in the banking research area and he remembered our earlier association favorably. Neil was an authoritative figure as he had a big build from his football days at Bucknell University and he was super competitive. In addition, he was an Irish Catholic in the traditional sense that he liked to drink in his youthful days. Rumor had it that he was an alcoholic in his early research years to deal with the stress as the first research director at the Federal Deposit Insurance Corporation (FDIC).

Upon learning of my University of Connecticut degree Neil supported my candidacy for an assistant professorship at VCU and vouched that I would be a good hire. Neil's support carried a lot of weight and I accepted the offer from VCU. I earned $59,500 my first year in 1989, and this was a salary that went far in the low wage South and City of Richmond, Virginia. It also worked out from a location standpoint as Janet and I were closer to her parents who had retired to Brookneal, Virginia. As an engineer, Janet was employable in almost any market and received a solid offer from a small engineering firm. Janet and I supported each other professionally, and there was never ever any jealousy in the pursuit of our happiness. We were a good team and the transition to Richmond was initially flawless. I settled into the Ivory Tower competition ready to win the hearts and minds of my colleagues as my prize.

My first year at VCU went very well and close to the plan. The primary responsibilities of a young assistant professor are to publish in the best academic journals possible, teach at a high level, and find a meaningful service mission that adds value for the university. I checked off the first box fairly easily as Neil took an interest in my research and we published a high-quality research paper in the Journal of Money Credit and Banking on technological change and the payments system. In the 1990s electronic transactions were just beginning to displace cash transactions at an alarming rate and having an impact on the velocity of money. Today the research paper is recognized as a one of the most cited articles on the payment system and a must-read paper on currency transactions. The administration upon hearing of the high-level publication liked to market the publication and the professor as it certified the quality of the University's research program for donors and grants. VCU had hired four assistant professors my first year and we had a natural competition. My initial high-quality publication essentially blew away the competition and I awaited the recognition of the Dean. One day I was walking down the hall proudly, and the Dean recognized me. We made eye contact, and I thought the Dean was going to congratulate me for my positive production. As the Dean approached, he said, "Ken I heard one of our young professors published in a good journal. Do you know what journal Professor Byles hit?"

Professor Byles was a hot-shot management professor from Oklahoma State University. Stunned by the Dean's assumptions that Professor Byles was the better talent, I replied, "No Dean Blanks, I have no information."

Dean Blanks was a long-time employee of the School of Business at VCU and was well liked. He had a strong Southern accent and did whatever the President wanted to advance the University. I smiled at Dean Blanks and quickly slid away from him after our short conversation. I had just felt my first slighted hand encounter in the Ivory Tower. I didn't let Dean Blanks know I was the young talented assistant professor, who had the quality publication, because it would create a very awkward moment for the two of us. In some strange way, I wanted to be invisible. I had endured so much racism in my academic experience such that it was more comfortable to accept less than I deserved some time because it allowed me to flow through the Ivory Tower without friction or direct harm. If I acknowledge Dean Blank's obvious error and omission then I would no longer be invisible and I would directly become a threat to his bigoted way of thinking. I was not looking to be a hero and be a social advocate for changing the Ivory Tower. I wanted to get tenure and support my family. In this sense I ironically desired a kind of invisible man experience described by Ralph Ellison. This admission of defeat from the Ivory Tower was the norm amongst most Black professors that looked to survive in the Ivory Tower. Most Black professors were not social activists like Mr. Ellison, looking to erase evil racism splattered across society. At VCU in our own meek way we were rattling the foundation of the Ivory Tower by just showing up every day and doing the hard work with no fanfare or obvious affinity for our contributions. My experiences such as the one with Dean Blanks would not be my last as the Ivory Tower. The Ivory Tower had a strong pecking order and there was an informal network of influence that interjected class, race and power into almost every decision made by the university.

I applied my strong work ethic and competitive attitude into my research and teaching at VCU. I was known as a difficult professor and my classes were known to be avoided if you were not a serious student. I took pride in my teaching and I truly believe I produced some top banking talent while at VCU. Several of my students got top banking jobs or competed well enough to get placed at the Federal Reserve Bank of Richmond.

Regardless of how good a teacher you are, it is well known that research pays the rent. My publication record in research stayed productive and consistent every year. Accordingly, I was promoted to the level of an associate professor of finance with tenure due to my positive record. Acquiring tenure is a rigor process that includes an independent evaluation external to the university along with an ad hoc internal evaluation process. Not many Black academics received promotion and tenure at VCU as the standards were extremely high. Racism almost always creeps into the advancement process. I was an external advisor for Lydia Tompkins, a Black Arts professor, who was denied tenure by the University president, Dr. Trani, even though her appeal process of discrimination along with her University appeals committee recommended she receive promotion and tenure. Such stories are common as many fiefdoms exist in the Ivory Tower at every level.

My ascent at VCU continued as I matured in my research, teaching and I even began a successful service program that landed me on four influential business boards in the past capital of the Confederacy, Richmond, Virginia. I was appointed to the State Treasury Board for consecutive terms by Governors Warner and Kaine, respectively. The State Treasury Board issued all state bonds for the Commonwealth of Virginia and also oversaw many of the state's financial programs such as the Tobacco Indemnification and Community Revitalization Endowment (TICR), which took the tobacco lawsuit settlements against the major cigarette makers and redeployed the funds into community investments in the Commonwealth of Virginia. I was also fortunate to attain the Board chairmanships of the Richmond Retirement System, a very large pension fund run by the City of Richmond, Virginia along with the Virginia Community Development Corporation (VCDC), the largest economic development corporation in the Commonwealth of Virginia. However, my crown jewel board appointment came as I was rewarded with a board seat on the Virginia Community Capital (VCC), a Denovo Bank. The VCC appointment was special because it was a private sector board seat with some small perks and a high-profile stature in my field of banking. Clearly, I was a top producer in my department and under any reasonable merit system I should have advanced within the department and the Ivory Tower. However, I did not advance as my skill level should have dictated. I watched as less talented White colleagues were selected for better paying and important positions as they played the Ivory Tower game to perfection. I knew of the Ivory Tower game but I wasn't well equipped to advance under an informal merit system that had no well designated rules. Failing to make the necessary adjustments to compete in the Ivory Tower I was content with my external service recognition and my high-end research program which earned me the rank of Professor of Finance.

As a Professor of Finance at VCU I held a selective position that was rarely achieved by a Black man or Black woman. I was the highest-ranking Professor in my department and out-classed my nearest department competitor, Dan Salandro in any relevant metric. Dan was a hard-working Italian from Pittsburgh who had a rugged exterior and wasn't the usual polished finance type of guy. However, Dan was very likeable because he was your typical "yes man" and he would brown nose or kiss anybody's ass to get his way or a job. I on the other hand was a prideful Black man who believed that results mattered and that in a meritocracy the best man wins. Boy was I wrong and I was about to get a life lesson in the complexity of racism in the Ivory Tower.

I will never forget the event because we had just hired a new dean, Ed Grier, from Disney and he was a Black man. I was excited and curious about how the arrival of such a high-profile Black professional would have on my career. Not only was I optimistic but almost every Black professional in the School of Business hoped that Dean Grier would correct the decades of injustice endured by Black men and Black women in the Ivory Tower. To be fair to Dean Grier he faced many constraints and the advancement of Black concerns above those by White faculty members may have made his job untenable. My advancement should have been a "no brainer" for Dean Grier but he showed no interest in my advancement or any significant minority issues, surprisingly. The lack of interest by Dean Grier was a shock to me as we got along well but his indifference surprised me and my Black colleagues at the university. Dean Grier's indifference begged the question,

Do Black executives ignore their Black professional colleagues intentionally to advance up the corporate ladder? Does the Ivory Tower and society at large expect successful Blacks to leave their brethren in the rear-view mirror as a prerequisite for their advancement? I did not have a clue about the answer to the questions I wanted to pose to Dean Grier. As you might imagine I felt it very ironic that after all my hard work that a Black man would be the vehicle to block my advancement. I was resigned to the fact that life was not fair in the Ivory Tower even when it had a Black prince.

The event which illuminated the complexity of racism by a Black dean in the Ivory Tower was the opening of the department chair position in the Finance, Insurance and Real Estate department in the VCU School of Business, my department. Most of my department colleagues felt I was the lead candidate for the position as there was no comparison to my colleague Dan Salandro. Dan had few quality publications and minimal management experience relative to me. However, the department chair hiring decision was done by an ad hoc committee selection process that included internal and external department committee members. This was an asset and flaw in the advancement of Black faculty members as outside faculty members could circumvent the merit hiring process by leaning on the strong internal networks established by the Ivory Tower culture. It took a strong Dean to understand the networking culture and to establish a culture of meritocracy to advance the plight of Black men and women in higher education.

Ironically, I knew everyone on the hiring committee well and got along well with them professionally for the most part. However, I would learn of their bias against me or I should say I learned of their bias against Black men and I just happened to be in their crosshairs. Ben Wier was one key hiring committee member and Ben was a nice guy. I played golf with Ben off campus and we got along well in general. In fact, my main research colleague worked with Ben and he gave me some key insights on Ben's motivation for being on the hiring committee. Ben's father was a former high-ranking army officer whose advancement in the Army had been derailed by the promotion of Colin Powell, a well-known Black General, to several key posts. It seems that Ben's father believed that Colin Powell had been advanced due to affirmative action at his expense. Ben told this story often and was clearly opposed to affirmative action. I knew of Ben's bias, but I had no inclination that it would be a hindrance to my application or my chance for the department chair position. This was just one barrier I had among the hiring committee members.

The second barrier I had was a junior faculty member that was appointed to the committee. Hiring committee members are supposed to not have any ethical or obvious conflicts of interest on the committee selection process. Dan Salandro had helped hire this junior faculty member and he was on the promotion and tenure committee for this same junior faculty member. Clearly this hiring committee member had a conflict of interest. I objected to the junior faculty member being placed on the committee to the School of Business Faculty council, but they claimed the process could only be altered by the Dean. At this point I was hoping Dean Grier would see such an obvious conflict of interest and intervene on my behalf. The intervention never occurred, and I was overlooked for the promotion in a close vote of 3 to 2. Two senior finance department members voted for me and 1 against me. Ironically, the department vote was determined more by the external votes than by the internal votes and Ben's vote was a major factor. More importantly, Dean Grier's inexperience and indifference played a large factor in the process. While some may have expected a fury of emotions from me after the decision, I was actually at peace because I had fought the good fight even though I had my reservations about my actual chances of winning the department chair. My father would have been proud, but he passed the week before and I willed myself through the interview. Even with memories of death and defeat on the job I could not muster a tear. After all these outcomes I did not think that life was cruel, it was just being a good teacher and preparing me for my next task. As I walked from VCU after not getting the department chair job, I thought of my long fast walks through my neighborhood to get to class or practice many years ago. I always got to class, and I always got to practice if I kept walking. VCU had put a significant roadblock in my advancement, now I just had to find a way to walk around it.

Looking back, I was clearly hurt by the event and it fueled my fire to increase my performance to illustrate the mistake made by the department and School of Business. The next year I had my best year professionally and my stature in the department increased significantly. I thought my professional development would be an asset by the department and school leaders. In hindsight my advancement only made them less secure as they had not achieved their advancement based on the merits. The same could also be said of Dean Grier. He came to academics as a private sector employee and never had done any academic research. The White faculty never truly respected him, and he was really an invisible man at a higher level. Although he may have wanted to help me advance, he was not able to support his fellow Black colleague due to the perception it may have created racial favoritism. This is a racist constraint placed on Black administrators in higher education or just a flexing of the muscles of White privilege in the Ivory Tower.

I got over the hiring of a clearly inferior candidate over me for the department chair and in some ways, it reinforced my core belief in not believing in the system. I did not believe in playing the Ivory Tower game as the odds were stacked against me and it was just proven to me. Also keep in mind that almost every person in my core finance department had uttered a racist comment to me or had exposed a racist view. Even my mentor Neil Murphy uttered some very insensitive remarks about my ancestors and slavery at a University of Virginia conference as we passed the old slave quarters. These facts show the complexity of racism as some very good people are imperfect individuals when it comes to navigating the sensitive subject.

I also began to feel that my core values did not match well with the university at this point in my career as the university was growing at an alarming rate at the expense of quality education. I started to plan my exit from the Ivory Tower. Also, I did not want to waste my experience any longer in an institutional setting that did not embrace my existence and contributions. I thank my Lord for his intervention for about a few years later I was given an exit strategy by the grace of God. What was the exit strategy? Initially my exit strategy was a bad one, but it did serve a purpose. As I got sick in my final year of working at VCU I was determined to never return to the classroom or academic research. I had watched many professors grow old and disgruntled due to the lack of meritocracy in the VCU management culture. I had so much to offer and I knew I could contribute to the world on a larger stage. My board work convinced me that I had the communication skills and talent to be an effective organizational leader. I had a brilliant mind and I was endowed with a gentle, kind character. I was proud of what I accomplished over my 30 year plus career at VCU and it was time to create my own organization for economic and social change. If I had not gotten sick, I do not think I would have never left VCU. The work came easy to me and life was comfortable in Richmond, Virginia with the legions of invisible men and women. However, God had a different plan for my time on Earth and it was up to me to execute His will. We all know the statement "To whom much is given much is required" but what is not required is to have all the answers all at once. What is required is a drive to not quit when the going gets tough and to roll with the punches when you get hit in the face. It reminded me of the statement I overheard by Coach Lester about me when I was in high school. He said, "I like that Daniels kid you can knock him around but you can't knock him down." VCU had knocked me around but the game was only beginning for me.

16

BLACK MAN ON BOARD

A UNIVERSITY EXPECTS TO make a meaningful contribution to its community through the service component of its mission and faculty workforce. The service component of a faculty member's possible work hours can be an internal university contribution such as serving on university committees like the faculty council or department service such as the promotion and tenure committee. These internal service opportunities are important as they are critical to the efficient operation of the university in a cost-effective way. If the university had to pay for this work and services by additional workers it would cost the university millions of dollars. Hence the university subsidizes its budget by shifting many tasks to the faculty at a reduced cost. Next there are external service opportunities that are highly visible and are almost like second jobs but they increase the stature of the university and they provide an important link to the community. External service opportunities can be of lesser importance, such as speaking at the rotary club, but most universities frown upon external service opportunities that are not value enhancing and they are not recognized as valuable in the promotion process of faculty members. At an early stage in my career, I recognized the value of external service opportunities and how they could be used to distinguish my career if I could land a spot on some influential finance boards at the state or national level that would increase my experience and supplement my managerial experience. I did not start seeking significant external service opportunities until after I had gotten tenure as an associate professor and most of my service opportunities as an assistant professor were of the internal service type.

All that would change one year when I met Greg Schnitzler, an adjunct faculty member in the finance department of VCU School of Business. Greg was a portfolio manager at the Treasury Department for the Commonwealth of Virginia. He was a kind soul and a great guy with vast experience from his days of living and working in New York as a finance professional. Greg was not your typical Richmond professional as he was conscious of its history and the need for the finance industry to reflect a broader set of the population. I do not know if this directive came from Mark Warner the new governor of the Commonwealth of Virginia or if Greg was just exercising his own commitment. Greg was helping the Treasury Board of Virginia cast a wider net to find qualified Board members for a seat on the State Treasury Board. The State Treasury Board was a high-profile office that helped the Commonwealth of Virginia finance its billion-dollar budget while maintaining an AAA credit rating which kept the interest cost of the state reasonable. By chance I had specialized in the area of municipal finance as an entry point into the finance literature as it was an area that was overlooked by the larger more prestigious finance departments in the country. Municipal bond research was looked upon as a secondary area of research and not as popular as equity or corporate debt financial research. Who would believe that a kid from East Orange would be one of the top municipal bond finance researchers in the entire United States of America? I didn't reach the designation alone as I worked closely with my colleague, VJ, in the accounting department and as a team we scoured the finance and accounting literature to find any angle to publish on municipal bonds. By the time I was an associate professor I had a well-established name and record in municipal finance research. Ironically, the municipal finance research area was just as large as the corporate debt market research but well-known finance scholars ignored its significance. This is currently changing as my research has brought the municipal finance market more attention and now more prestigious universities are trying to corner the municipal finance area. However, back in the 1990s the Black University of Connecticut PhD had established himself as a solid researcher and people took notice. My name got passed along to Greg Schnitzler and we briefly met. He told me of the opportunities of serving on the Treasury Board and how I might contribute. Our meeting and discussion were cordial as he asked me to forward my vita to him. On arriving back at my office, I submitted my vita but had no expectation of hearing from Greg again. Months went by after the meeting and I had not heard anything from Greg or anyone about my submission for serving on the Treasury Board for the Commonwealth of Virginia. Then one morning I got an interesting email from the Secretary of the Governor. You can tell when an email is important. It was an official looking document from the Commonwealth of Virginia as it was marked as important in our email system. In the 1990s email was becoming the primary method of communication above letter writing commonly known as snail mail. Curiously, I opened the email and it read "Dear Dr. Daniels". It continued "I would like to congratulate you on your appointment to the Treasury Board for the Commonwealth of Virginia ". A sudden burst of pride filled my chest as I had been selected to a professional position of influence based on my intellectual prowess and hard work. Fifteen years before I hardly knew what a municipal bond was in the field of finance.

More importantly, it showed that the system of personnel selection worked in the system of state government unlike the Ivory Tower at VCU. It was a time to soak in some air of self-appreciation and a self-pat on the back because no one in my department or the School of Business would recognize my achievement formally or informally. This pattern would repeat itself as I continued to receive external recognition. When I got home and told Janet of the great news of my appointment to the Treasury Board she responded, "That's nice."

I think Janet just thought the appointment to the Treasury Board was just another university type committee as she did not quite grasp the business aspect of government and the university. I put my bags on the counter and walked briskly out to my garden. Even if the university and my wife did not promote my accomplishments, my garden always welcomed me home in good times or bad.

My next board appointment of significance was the Virginia Community Development Corporation (VCDC). VCDC was the largest economic development corporation in the Commonwealth of Virginia and Virginia's oldest manager of tax credit equity funds. VCDC brought together developers, investors, and communities to build affordable rental housing and revitalize historic properties. VCDC also manages multi-investor and proprietary equity investment funds that provide development capital mainly through the use of Low-Income Housing Tax Credits (LIHTC), Historic Tax Credits, and New Markets Tax Credits. As you can see from the above statements that VCDC had a complicated and expansive mission that was important to keeping Virginia's neighborhood vibrant and expanding. I was proud to serve on its board as the work was important in minority neighborhoods.

The way that I got connected with VCDC was kind of funny as it came through a social setting with one of Janet's business partner's Robert Easter. Robert was a minority architect in Richmond, Virginia and a family friend. Janet worked often with Robert on his architectural and design projects. On this night Robert invited us to a comedy dinner show on the Southside of Richmond and he also invited some of his business clientele. Part of his entourage was some staff members from VCDC as they often recommended Robert as a good architect to use on projects. The dinner show was really funny and everyone was talkative and having a good time. I happened to sit by Arild from VCDC and he was a key administrator and head of investor relations. VCDC raised a lot of capital, primarily from banks, to invest in housing. As a reward for the use of their capital banks got lower tax liabilities and investors got below market rates of capital. The financing of VCDC's portfolios were unique and I started an interesting conversation with Arild. We hit it off pretty good as I understood most of the concepts, he discussed the inner workings of VCDC. Arild inquired about my background and I told him I was a Professor of Finance. He was intrigued and asked me if I would be interested in talking to the chief executive officer (CEO) of VCDC Ralph Nodine. I said, "Sure, why not?"

Arild smiled and we went back to laughing about the comedy show. In a few seconds I had a connection to the VCDC and its CEO. Little did I know that I would take a leadership role with VCDC over the years as I found a mentor and friend in Ralph Nodine.

Ralph Nodine was a unique personality and a talented professional who had mastered the art of public finance and tax credits. This field of study is not well known and it is so complicated that you cannot use ordinary accountants to audit the complicated liability companies that house the assets and liabilities of VCDC. Only a few specialized accountants will take on the work at substantial fees because the risk is significant. Ralph was well connected and had worked with Governor Wilder during his administration to set up most of the tax credit programs in the Commonwealth of Virginia. Ralph had retired from the field of public finance and was living in Maine when I met him. He was called back to work at VCDC by the state of Virginia to ensure that the organization was well established and headed in the right direction.

I got a phone call from Ralph at my office and he introduced himself as Ralph. He said, "Ken, this is Ralph."

I asked, "Ralph who?"

Ralph chuckled on the phone and said, "Well, I guess a big professor like you wouldn't know who I am." I had to laugh at Ralph as I quipped, "If I was really that big, I wouldn't be talking to you."

Needless to say, Ralph and I hit off immediately. I was comfortable with him and he was comfortable with me as I had no agenda to circumvent anyone's power on the board. Ralph suggested we meet for breakfast at Perly's, a popular Richmond breakfast spot where all the power brokers met to discuss business. We arranged a time and I met Ralph for breakfast where he discussed his concerns and how I might be able to help. He told of the changing landscape of tax financing and how the arrangements were becoming more sophisticated and finance based. He illustrated a few portfolios and he then indicated that most of his board did not really understand the structure of the activities of VCDC nor did they understand the risk that was being generated. Ralph wanted to change the capability of the board so that there was better oversight and less risk of mismanagement. Also, he made it clear that he wanted to retire to Maine as soon as he had the shop in good shape. As I looked at Ralph, I felt that I had another stroke of good luck as I had another White male that respected my ability and was entrusting me with some real responsibility. Although I had some stature at VCU, the White power structure made it real clear that I was to stay in my lane and not really look for any advancement. Advancement at VCU was down in smoke-filled rooms or by donors who had influence.

In Ralph, I saw another opportunity to advance my name based on the merits and it succeeded. I immediately helped VCDC by expending a lot of time monitoring activities appropriately on the investment committee or audit committee. These activities took time and could not be done haphazardly as they would eventually be monitored and audited down to the penny. Things had to be watched and tough questions had to be asked. Ralph watched as I did the work and asked the hard questions and got results to his satisfaction. Ralph eventually promoted me to Chairman of the Board of VCDC. He jokingly said the reason he gave me the opportunity was because my resume needed some help. Although Ralph made light of the situation, his confidence in me led to many more opportunities. I respected Ralph tremendously as he showed me how a confident manager delegates but maintains control through respect for the individual and the organization. These were management skills and project management skills that the typical professor never learns or never gets the opportunity. Ralph opened my eyes to so much and he did it in a professional management way which was so counterintuitive to the Ivory Tower way. My work at VCDC pumped some fresh air back into my system and made me believe in people and organizations again.

My board work at VCDC led to another board position which was a bank called Virginia Community Capital. VCDC was an independent organization of the state but it was heavily influenced by the political power structure at the state level. This was because the historical tax credit portfolio was a state-owned portfolio and it had been gifted to VCDC under the Wilder administration to create a statewide economic development corporation. Governor Warner was now the lead politician in the state during my time at VCDC and he had a novel idea to start a state financed bank that was focused on underdeveloped markets. This new bank would be called Virginia Community Capital (VCC) and it was established by merging some pledge assets from VCDC, along with a $15 million capital injection into the Denovo Bank by the Commonwealth of Virginia. As a reward for its pledge assets VCDC got one board seat on the newly formed bank which was a very high-profile institution given its risk and mission. Hearing of the newly formed bank at a VCDC board meeting I just assumed that Ralph would assume the seat because he had the reputation to demand respect on such a board and he would protect the interest of VCDC appropriately. One day I got a phone call from Ralph and he immediately said, "Ken, how are you?"

I replied, "I am fine Ralph. How are you?"

Ralph gleefully replied, "When I am in Maine and not on a plane to Richmond, I am fine."

Now I knew Ralph's motivation for not seeking the board seat with VCC. Ralph wanted to retire to Maine as soon as possible and enjoy his well-deserved retirement.

He continued, "Ken, how would you like to fill the board seat at Virginia Community Capital?"

I was silent on the phone as being a bank board member was in another league from my public board responsibilities. First, you had to have a financial stake in the private entity through a stock purchase and the time commitment would be tremendous. I was already on two boards and could I fill a third board commitment responsibly. Finally, I said to Ralph, "Can I think about it and get back to you soon?"

He said, "Ken, that's a good idea. Sleep on it and I'll call you tomorrow, but I think you would be great for the position."

I appreciated Ralph's patience and his vote of confidence. Opportunities like this did not come around every day. I went home and talked to Janet about the opportunity and she seemed to support whatever I decided on. I did not tell her that I would have to buy $5,000 of VCC stock as I am sure that would have changed her mind. Janet thought all my money was the family's money and would see my opportunity as taking away from something for her or the kids. Her potential argument may have had some merit but this was my time to shine. In the morning, I called Ralph back and said, "Ralph, I am in and thank you for the opportunity."

Quietly Ralph said, "Ken, you'll do great and thank you for serving."

We both hung up the phone relatively quickly as there was no small talk about Maine or the weather or the kids. Ralph had passed the baton to me and I grabbed it confidently without reservation. I was entering my prime and it felt good.

My first board meeting with VCC was strange. VCC was a newly formed bank and we met at the headquarters of Bank of America downtown as VCC had no facilities. At the initial meeting were former bank CEO, Sandy Fitzhugh and the Bank of America President of Virginia. The Fitzhughs were an old Richmond family that had a street in Richmond named after them. I had something in common with Sandy as his grandkids attended Collegiate School in the West End. Also, on the board was Bill Shelton who was a well-respected state community development specialist and a close confidant of Governor Warner. Michael Schewel, Secretary of Trade and Commerce in Governor Warner's administration, was also on the board. Mike's family was well-established in Virginia business and the family furniture business in Lynchburg, Virginia. As you can see, the board had a lot of competent and respected professionals and then there was me. I didn't exactly fit the mold of the Denovo Bank board member but banking is where I cut my teeth as a professional banker in Springfield, Massachusetts, where I worked as an asset liability manager. I knew everything about bank financial reporting and regulation. My main professional experience came while working at the Old Bank of New England as I was the main analyst in the finance department for the bank. Needless to say, although I didn't look the part, I had more practical knowledge than anyone in the room and I was determined to show it. Finally, the meeting started and Sandy Fitzhugh had everyone introduce themselves and then he said, "Let me call into the room the chief executive officer of VCC, Jane Henderson."

Into the room waltzed a tall, slender, attractive woman who looked the part of a banking professional. Jane Henderson had risen through the ranks of Wachovia bank as a community banking executive but had a solid management record and was hand-picked for the job by Mark Warner and his inner circle. She ran the board meeting flawlessly and was approachable as a person. Jane had brought VCC to life and she was ready for her moment to return to the banking world. Rumor had it that she retired early from Wachovia due to some disagreements with senior management but I was never ever able to confirm the rumors.

I initially had a very good relationship with Jane. We were all learning on the fly as this was the first nonprofit community development financial institution (CDFI) as a holding company that owned a for profit bank. Very simple the bank took on all the low-risk bankable assets and the CDFI took on more risk and financed the soft cost of human capital development which was non-recoverable most of the time. Initially Jane made a bunch of bad hires as her asset liability team, and I was constantly correcting their mistakes as a board member on the asset liability committee. It got so bad that Jane fired one of the asset liabilities managers and informally offered me the job. I don't know if she was serious or not but she was frustrated and a little bit in over her head as a CEO initially. However, she quickly recovered and drove asset growth and profitability in the right direction. As a board member, I was a little dismayed with some of the direction of VCC in terms of its commitment to development in minority communities and I had no confidence that the other board members saw minority community development as a critical issue. This issue came to a head one board meeting when Jane began reporting development by region and it became clear that any region with significant minority populations had lower activity. Michael Schewel noticed the lower activity and saw it as a negative and recommended that we just delete the information. Immediately this caught my ire and I responded by saying it was wrong to not report our deficiency in minority lending. I was out-voted on the issue and it became clear to me that VCC was not really a vehicle that could infuse much needed capital into the troubled minority communities of Virginia. As time went on, I became more disillusioned with the management of VCC. The numbers look great but a closer look showed that the mission was still not being met. Today, VCC is an $800 million institution leveraged from a $15 million investment.

On the surface, it should be a model for the nation but everyone knows that minority business is not properly funded in Virginia and across the nation. VCC was supposed to be part of the answer. To be fair to Jane, there are significant risk capital restrictions on the banking side and serious regulatory gaps on the CDFI side which make her attempt encumbered. I enjoyed my time at VCC, but I know I could have contributed more if the management was open to my ideas. Before I retired, Jane brought in a Black PhD in management from the University of Virginia that had some research and ideas on minority business lending. I did not take him seriously, and I do not think he has made much of a difference. I took his ascension on the board as a signal that it was time for me to leave. I quietly left VCC when I got sick and was not able to make the meetings even by phone. I received a nice plaque from Jane and the board which was a kind act. The people on the VCC board and management team are fine people but they have no clue how to interject capital deep into Black neighborhoods. I hope in the future that I will be able to address this issue in depth as my final act in my professional career.

Finally, I was also appointed to the Richmond Retirement Board by the City of Richmond. This is ironic because years before my appointment, my good buddy was the City Manager of Richmond and I hinted at being appointed to the pension fund board for the city. Calvin, my Black City Manager buddy, also made big promises but never followed through and I never heard from him about the appointment. I got recommended to be on the City of Richmond Retirement Board because Greg Schnitzler was again involved in the process and he recommended my name to Ron Tillet, the board chairman. Ron Tillet was the former Secretary of Finance of the Commonwealth of Virginia and served as State Treasurer of the Commonwealth of Virginia. Ron was a confident, boisterous character, and I got along well with him and I rose in responsibility at the Richmond Retirement Board as I viciously defended the fund from poor performance by investment managers. Investment managers are always trying to schmooze the board or slide their results by lazy monitors of the fund. I nipped this in the bud as I was prepared every meeting to ask the tough questions that needed to be asked. Ron appreciated my hard work and eventually groomed me to be the Board Chairman of the Retirement Fund. Ron also had done enough service for the City along with the Commonwealth of Virginia, and was looking to work more in the private sector. I appreciated Ron just like I appreciated Ralph. Although I didn't become friends with Ron, I learned from his management style and his dedication to respect people and the organization. Ron was also more of a political animal than Ralph but I had no appetite to venture down the political lane. If I had followed Ron's suggestions to get involved more politically, I could have risen more in the political and business arena of the state capital.

As I look back, every young professional like myself was trying to leverage their wares into a better employment position from their political appointments and their business networks. I was happy to teach, do my research, and attend my board meetings to stay away from the foray into the payola game. In my mind, I always had my integrity and no one could ever say that they paid for Dr. Ken Daniels with money or in-kind contribution. The ascension up the professional playing field is not a free lunch. You must be in the game and be willing to play the game with intention to succeed and keep your peace of mind. I do not know many that play the game well as there is always a price to pay. Even when you do not play the game, the consequences follow your actions and track you down. In my case, I could retreat to my garden, my pond, and if I had the backing of my family, I wouldn't have had a care in the world.

I think my experience as a board member and specifically a Black board member illuminates some of the challenges that are faced by Black professionals. In my case, I was always promoted by an experienced White professional that had my best interest at heart. Without a Ralph, a Greg or a Ron there is no significant board experience for Dr. Ken Daniels. These champions, and I truly believe they are champions, got no direct reward for their professional acts of kindness and they may even have caused some friction by overlooking some White privilege candidate. Ralph, Greg and Ron were ahead of their time and society needs more champions to level the playing field and increase more opportunity. Notice that I do not put Jane in the champion's camp, even though she promoted Greg, the Black faculty member. She did not facilitate a better environment and a more effective organization in my opinion. I know Jane has been very effective in gender advancement and promoting women in the VCC organization but the example where Jane was co-opted into not being transparent about minority business activity illuminated her true stance which is unacceptable in my book. I hope I am wrong about Jane and that she turns her performance around at VCC.

As the events of 2020 have shown and the *Black Lives Matter* movement signal, the world is now demanding better performance from organizations like VCC. Our failure to deliver effective results will have significant consequences for Black people for generations.

17

ENAYA AND THE QURAN

AS ONE GOES THROUGH a spiritual awakening it is natural to seek the companionship of our Lord and his manifestation through religion on earth. I was brought up as a conservative Baptist with strong emphasis on the reconstruction or rebirth of the soul through a symbolic baptism. The baptism in spirit represented a cleansing of the soul by God's hand and it was a common belief that one cannot enter heaven without this spiritual cleansing by God.

Although I was a self-proclaimed Baptist I have never been baptized by a minister. As such I self-identified with the religion but had serious doubts about the religion as a fit for me. It was during the time of my illness and shortly after that I began an investigation into Islam as a religion for me. I began my investigation of Islam by taking an Arabic class at VCU. The Arabic class was supposed to be a casual conversational Arabic class given by the University to encourage continuous learning. However, it turned out to be the Arabic class from hell as I landed on an Arabic teacher from Lebanon that was insistent that we learn to read, write and converse in Arabic fluently over the 6-week class. The university provided a class incentive that if you received a B then the university paid for the class therefore making the class essentially free. However, if you did not receive a B then you owed the university $300. Everyone in the Arabic class was in a panic by the fourth class as the instructor was coming to class with homework and instructions for assignments to be done by the next class. I had a rigorous research agenda during the time and I started to get anxious about the amount of time required for the supposedly easy conversational class. I began the class with hesitation but then the beauty of the Arabic language grabbed my attention. I played with the artful symbols of the Arabic alphabet while the Arabic reading of right to left stimulate d me mentally. I found Arabic fun and I let some of my research assignments slip due to the intrigue. I was not the only student that gravitated to the rigorous approach of the female teacher from Lebanon. Her demeanor was always serious but she had an agenda of teaching Arabic to get the student to respect the language. I had a feeling that her hidden message was that you had to respect the Arabic language to respect the Arabic people. If you took this logic further than the casual investigation of Arabic by Americans was disrespectful and did not give the proper attention to understanding a language. In addition, the command of Arabic opens up a world of non-Western knowledge along with access to billions of people. Muslims and their religion Islam.

I met Enaya on the internet as I was preparing for one of my trips to Australia. During my time at VCU, I had been to Australia three times and I was fascinated by the continent and its people. I was interested in the Australian Aboriginals who belong to the Australoid race. The history of Australoid race in Australia intrigued me as the government was willing to come to grips with the past transgressions of genocide and racism. This provided an opportunity for finance research to develop specialized institutions to support the Australian Aboriginals. I met a couple of Australian researchers interested in my idea and they thought there was potential. I used my conference trips to Australian to learn about the Australian Aboriginal and became fascinated by their art which is a unique painting technique using dots.

The art of Australian Aboriginals and the dot technique is an imported technique from Indonesia. This cultural connection illustrated the unique complex relationship the country of Australia had with its Asian neighbors and China. Indonesia had an influential impact on Australia through the spice trade and a natural cultural exchange developed between Indonesia and Australia as a byproduct. Enaya was Indonesian and her family was an influential family in Indonesian history and the development of trade between Australia and Indonesia. Our initial conversations were quite innocent as they focused on the history of Indonesians in Australians and her family history. I found this fascinating as it opened an Eastern way of thinking which was so contrary to Western philosophy. Enaya's father was of Chinese descent and an early philosopher in Indonesian folklore. Enaya would tell these elegant stories of the beauty of the Indonesian people and the education of tribal Indonesia as it grew as a country and an exporter of spices and culture across Asia. The beauty of the Indonesian people was definitely passed along to Enaya as she was a beautiful woman with relatively darker skin along with Cleopatra's figure, sharp mind and an intriguing funny personality. Enaya lived in Australia and their time zone was approximately 14 hours ahead. I would go to the office early in the morning and Enaya would be finishing up her work day and this technological connection through the internet made our relationship possible. Every morning I would turn on my computer and Enaya would be there just hanging out talking to people on the internet and exchanging concepts and ideas. I soon started conversing with Enaya and we clicked as my interest in Eastern culture and her interest in Western culture provided an opportunity for cross cultural collaboration. We hit it off immediately and the internet now allowed video communication such that I could see Enaya and she could see me. To understand my relationship with Enaya you need to understand that we talked for about 2 years to each other almost every morning before we met as she lived almost on the other side of the Earth. At the time, I did not consider this cheating as it was impossible to meet Enaya while I was in America. I have since learned and agree that true commitment requires that all emotional attachment be a singular focus on the love of your life.

On one of my conference visits to Australian, I met Enaya and we talked but she was busy with work in Melbourne such that we only had time for coffee. When I first met Enaya, it was very awkward and she looked like a school kid as she talked to me. Even though we had talked together often online, I could tell she was very uncomfortable meeting me in person and talking. However, my initial visit with Enaya confirmed my intuition about her. She had a royal looking feel to her and she was majestic in her movements. More importantly, I could learn from Enaya the Eastern knowledge from her background in a very unassuming and unique way which intrigued me. We were sipping coffee at the cafe when Enaya said something that surprised me. She said, "You know Ken, you look Indonesian."

I chuckled, "Really."

I bluntly told Enaya I was a pure blooded African American male. She said, "I know. I have read all about Malcolm X and Martin Luther King."

Enaya was special and she had a cultural affinity for the history of Black Americans. She began to tell me of the struggles of the Indonesian people and how it mimicked the struggles of Blacks in America. I consumed everything Enaya said as it expanded my knowledge of a new world and opened my mind to possible work opportunities. Enaya was a recent divorcee and she talked briefly about her husband but gave a dissertation when talking about her sons. Enaya and I talked the afternoon away before she left. I had no real reason to see Enaya again as I went to my conference and flew back to the USA.

My trip to Australia was a success. My paper on *clawbacks*, a type of debt to equity conversion process for corporations, was well received. I bought some nice Aboriginal art that cemented my interest in the Australoid race and I met Enaya. When I got back to my office at VCU, there was an electronic message from Enaya through the video messaging system. I didn't think anything of the message as I opened it and expected the usual *nice to meet you* correspondence. To my surprise the message went in a different direction as Enaya expressed her emotions upon meeting me. In the message, Enaya said she thought of me since we met. She also proclaimed that I reminded her of a good-looking Indonesian man and that I would look good in traditional Indonesian garb. She apologized for her awkward uneasiness towards me as she wanted me to know that the uneasiness came from some hidden unintentional emotion that we had acquired for each other. Finally, Enaya mentioned that she was a Muslim and wanted me to know her religion. As I sat in my office chair, a warm glow came over me as I thought of this beautiful Indonesian woman and her affection for me. Of course, I was attracted to Enaya but I didn't want to make a wrong move and scare her away. Apparently, my reserved approach to her struck a chord, and now we had something else to talk about during our video conferencing.

Falling in love is an event that does not happen quickly and requires time. Falling in love can happen unexpectedly and the heart can become a dominating character who cannot be controlled. I did not try or expect to fall in love with Enaya. It just happened over a long time period and I probably fell in love with the idea of her before I fell in love with her. As Enaya answered my ping for my morning call, after reading her message, her smile jumped out of the computer and wrapped around my brain. Enaya was so infectious that I could not control my desire for her now that the cat was out of the bag. I said, "Good morning."

She chuckled, "You know, it's evening here Ken."

Enaya was physically on the other side of the world but her spirit was already inside my soul and growing. I continued, "I was surprised by your message."

Enaya got serious and she interjected, "Ken, ever since my divorce, it has been hard for me to look at men."

Enaya's divorce had been hard on her since it removed her from a lot of the institutional benefits her husband received. Her ex-husband was a high-ranking Indonesian patriot and received significant perks as he partitioned out the access to the Indonesian people and its economy to the corporations of the world. I responded, "Enaya you don't owe me any explanation about your situation. I just love having you as a friend."

Enaya did not say anything but just beamed at me with her radiant beauty. Enaya then said, "Ken, I wasn't going to see you again. I know you are married and I am Muslim, but something about your smile stuck with me and I had a dream about you as a Muslim man."

Enaya had just let me into her world and she was confident enough to let me know that I crossed her mind and maybe as a possible partner. I was not aware of the unique intricacies of the Muslim faith at the time nor did I know much about Muslim women. Trying to get a grasp of what Enaya and I were talking about I said, "Enaya, I must admit that I am extremely attracted to you but you live on the other side of the world. Do you think you would ever come to the United States to live or to see me?"

Enaya paused for a second and said, "Ken, I expect I could live anywhere in the world for the right man, but I would expect that he would be a Muslim and want to get to know my family in Indonesia and Australia."

In a few seconds, Enaya had given me the road map and a new way to think of my relationship with her. Enaya continued with her usual funny self and chuckled at me saying, "Plus you are good looking and I want to see you in a batik."

I said, "What is a batik?"

"A batik was a type of formal shirt with intricate Indonesian patterns that distinguished the region."

Enaya continued to expand my mind to a new culture, a new way of thinking, and eventually a new religion.

As you might imagine, Islam took on a larger role and novel place in my education with my evolving relationship with Enaya. I had finished my Arabic class at VCU, and Enaya was amazed about how much Arabic I had learned in a short period of time. I could write full Arabic sentences and understand them. Although I had ventured to learn Arabic, I had not taken a step towards Islam or becoming a Muslim. This changed one day when Enaya sent me a beautiful Quran. It was a large book and it was nicely crafted. The Quran has many surahs and I started to read them with great interest and found some comfort is the readability of the surahs. What was Enaya's intent by sending me a Quran? Was it just a kind act or a motivated action to stroke my exploration of the soul? Did Enaya want to be a part of my life or just a long-distance friend of some sort? These are the questions which ran through my head with no answers but I had plenty to do with a full agenda.

As I started to read the Quran, I felt a natural connection to the readings. I grew in profound ways which included better hygiene, better eating habits, and an awareness of my connection to mankind. The teachings were relatively simple but had great lessons of right and wrong in common dealings with your fellow man. It was almost like a life road map for every instance one could conceive of encountering. I had my own special circumstance with a Muslim woman interested in me and a wife who was always busy with her company. I can remember as Janet discovered my interest in Islam and commented, "It's nice you are learning about Islam but I didn't marry no Muslim."

I was stunned that she would not love me unconditionally and even put some guardrails on what I could believe. Despite Janet's reservation, I continued my study and reading of the Quran. Enaya on the other hand was very encouraging of my study of the Quran and I would ask her stupid questions on the faith. She would always be patient and kind in her tutelage. She also informed me that she was keeping her commitment to Islam and looking forward to Hajj. Hajj is a pilgrimage to the holiest city to cleanse the soul and bring Muslims together. Enaya and I were almost at opposite ends of the spectrum of our understanding of the Quran where she was advanced and I a beginner. How could two people in different places in the world and different places on the values curve come to a common place of understanding? Love is a unique force that bonds the unbendable and makes the undoable doable almost effortlessly.

I started getting more serious about Enaya as Janet and I just drifted in our marriage. Janet was going through some financial difficulty with her firm and was spending a tremendous amount of time at the office. I was consumed by my work also and spent a lot of time alone after work. My relationship with Enaya filled a cavern in my life in so many ways, and we would talk hours away. First, Enaya was a spiritual guide to me as she explained my questions on the practical implementation of Islam and prayer. Second, Enaya was a good friend and cared for my well-being and my troubles at work, home or life. Third, Enaya and I were growing closer to love. I do not know how to explain my connection to Enaya physically or sexually as I had never kissed her or touched her. The distance between us almost made our connection surreal.

Once Janet left me during my illness, I was on my own and I never assumed I would go right to Enaya. First, I was really ill and my illness took some time to get over. This lapse in time disconnected me from Enaya and an immediate chance of a love connection. I was not able to travel until the early part of 2017. Second, Enaya lived in Australia, and we would have to plan any visit because of the distance and the logistics. After the divorce and the early part of 2017, I relocated to New Jersey to get away from Virginia and try to get myself together. I contacted Enaya to let her know I was divorced and maybe now was a good time to meet. She agreed and we decided to meet in Singapore as it was a halfway point and receptive to Western culture. I was excited that Enaya wanted to meet as the short absence did not disrupt our chemistry. I had mixed feelings about meeting Enaya as she was a Muslim and she had conveyed her desire or wish to be with a Muslim man. I was not a Muslim and I was trying to get close to a Muslim woman. Clearly, I had a dilemma on my hands. At least I did not have to feel guilty about cheating on Janet as the divorce cleared my conscience to follow my heart. Enaya and I talked regularly to get reacquainted and to plan our visit. Amazingly, Enaya took the lead on the accommodations and made the logistics of the trip very easy. Essentially, I just had to book a flight and show up. As we planned the trip, Enaya asked some probing questions about my study of the Quran. Not probing in an evasive sense but just checking to see that I was still engaged in Islam. I had read the Quran three times by this point as I had ample time on my hands and was not doing research anymore. In a way my reading of the Quran transitioned me away from hard core technical research as I had an important assignment to find a vehicle for my soul. Was Islam a religion I could embrace to find comfort or was Islam a necessary requirement to be with Enaya? Clearly, the answer to the latter is yes, but I struggled to find comfort in Islam. In fact, quite the contrary as I got closer to going to a mosque or my interaction with Muslims, I felt a sense of urgency or anxiety.

To give you an example of my anxiety with Islam, as I was juxtaposed with the religion, came from my regular visits to the Seven Eleven for coffee.

Every morning, I would go to the Seven Eleven for coffee to start my day. The store was close to where I lived and I would mindlessly drive there every morning to get my day started. The coffee brought some relief and the daily visits stimulated me through some social interaction. One of the key interactions was with the store clerk. I don't remember his name but he was of Arabic descent. I overheard him speaking Arabic as I checked out with my coffee and I naturally said, "Shukran," which meant *thank you* in Arabic.

He looked at me in a funny way and said, "How do you know Arabic?"

I smiled and said, "I know," and walked out the store.

I could feel his eyes follow me to the car and I went on my way. The next day I went to the Seven Eleven and I had a more detailed discussion with the clerk. We chatted aimlessly at first then I asked, "Are you Muslim?"

Sensing a focus of my inquiry he said, "I am a Muslim in America, and being a Muslim here is hard."

Not expecting such an answer, I probed further and asked, "What is so difficult about being a Muslim here?"

He immediately replied, "There are not many Muslims here and we have a real tiny Mosque."

I was interested in Islam and how local Muslims practiced their religion but I didn't push any further with my questions. We ended our conversation there as I drank my coffee and headed out the store. I had many conversations with the clerk over the next few weeks discussing Islam and his faith. He sensed my desire for knowledge but I kept a comfortable distance as our conversations were always brief and I was passing through, never stopping for a full engagement. Then one day, he physically stopped me and started a conversation. He said, "I went to the Mosque and I told the Imam about you."

Given that we had never really had a direct conversation, I was taken aback by his stance. I answered, "Why did you do that?"

He said, "The Imam is interested in you and you should visit the Mosque."

Immediately I sensed a fear of a trap. I do not know any other way to explain it. The clerk had done nothing wrong and he was kind in his invitation. Did I overreact in a bigoted way or were my innate senses

No Tears

accurate? Sidestepping the clerk, I said, "Shukran," paid for my coffee and left the store.

Feeling uneasy about the encounter, I questioned my senses and wondered if I had been rude to the clerk. Would I have reacted the same way if he was a Christian and he invited me to meet his pastor? Whether a Muslim or Christian, I thought the approach was aggressive and it sent off an unknown alarm inside of me. I never went back to the Seven Eleven for coffee again and I started a new daily routine to claim my normalcy.

As I boarded the plane, I kept an open mind about my reunion with Enaya with no expectations. The flight to Singapore was long since there were not any direct flights, and I had two stops on the way. I usually did not mind layovers as it allowed me time to see different places and to gauge how far American infrastructure was behind the rest of the world. During my travels, I have seen beautiful airports in France, Portugal, Australia, Vancouver, and Greece for example. The architectural design of the foreign airports is usually superior and the infrastructure is up to date. As I landed in Singapore, I was blown away by the modern infrastructure and the cleanliness of the public areas. Comparing the USA infrastructure to Singapore was not even fair. Although Singapore has a smaller location and economy, it was clear that much thought, planning, and effort had gone into its transportation system. I quickly got my bags and headed off to the hotel.

I met Enaya at the Hotel Sofitel in Singapore. Enaya had raved about this hotel, and I had never heard of the brand. Well the hotel did not disappoint as it was massive and amazing. It was very functional but they treated all guests like a prime minister from check in to check out. The hotel was located in a very high-end district but you could walk to the beach down a steep hill. I remember the hill as Enaya and I held hands walking down the hill to the beach. But I am getting ahead of myself, let me backtrack and take you back to Enaya meeting me at the hotel in Singapore.

As I rode the shuttle van up to the hotel, I was exhausted after a 29-hour trip. I rang Enaya about my arrival, and I waited in the lobby for her to come get me. I was in awe of the hotel as I viewed its architecture and infrastructure. The lobby had a sort of outdoor indoor feel as the climate promoted a spacious surrounding. As I turned around, I saw Enaya gliding toward me in a flowing light-colored Arabic garb. The scarf over her shoulders flew in the wind of her walk as again she promoted a majestic view or maybe I was just smitten with her. Reaching out with both hands she said, "Ken, you made it."

I took her words literally as the kid from East Orange felt like he had made it. I grabbed Enaya's hands as she swung her arm around my waist and we walked to the room. As we walked, she pointed to the little fish in a pond and said, "If you want Ken, you can get a pedicure here."

I thought she was kidding but later I would find hotel guests sitting by the beautiful pool with their feet in the water. Little catfish would smell your feet and come eat the dead skin off your feet. The little catfish did an incredible job. Enaya and I turned the corner and strolled down a long corridor catching up about our travel and a few local attractions we wanted to see. As we approached the room door, I almost had to pinch myself to make sure it wasn't a dream. Here I was with the woman of my dreams smiling at me getting ready to enter a hotel room. Looking up at me, Enaya smiled and kissed me on the cheek before we entered the room.

I don't want to be naïve, but I don't think there was any doubt that Enaya and I were going to make love in Singapore. Our physical attraction was off the charts and emotions can be controlled but I am not so sure real love can be contained. At least I thought Enaya and I had a chance at a long loving relationship that would lead to marriage. Enaya and I had talked a lot before Singapore, and we both indicated our intentions for a long-term relationship. Enaya and I sat on the bed when we got in the room and she gave me a big hug along with a kiss. Then we began to talk about our relationship and Enaya began to talk about me coming to Sydney to be with her.

Clearly, Enaya was indicating that our relationship would be centered in Sydney and Jakarta. She had two lovely homes and a lot of investment real estate but her business interests were not anywhere near the USA. I could get a university position almost anywhere in the world but with limitations. I was intrigued with the idea of leaving the USA but the discussion did seem premature to me. I did not let on to Enaya about my reservations but just followed her lead. Next, Enaya dove right into the conversion to Islam for me. First keep in mind that Islam has been around me all my life since high school as my two best friends were practicing Muslims. I had been to the Mosque several times with them and my younger brother, Kyle, had been a Muslim but he later rejected Islam. As for me I enjoyed reading the Quran and I had thought of converting to Islam but at best I was a passive believer of Islam. Even when I identified as a Baptist, I didn't attend church often. Islam is an active religion of practicing rituals and doing a pilgrimage if you can make it happen. Enaya was an active believer in Islam and growing in her spirituality. I even kidded with her about having five wives to knock her back on her belief. She did not budge an inch about my right but said be careful that you can take care of each one. I embraced Islam as a part of Enaya. I wanted Islam to help the both of us ground our union on a solid foundation. Our discussion was healthy and I didn't feel pressured by Enaya as I was seeking my own spiritual growth and Islam was the option, I was exploring to grow my soul. We ended up agreeing that I would take it slow where maybe I would convert to Islam if I moved to Sydney. Exhausted after the trip along with a deep conversation Enaya and I laid down together in an affectionate spooning position and fell asleep together. I was as happy as can be as I drifted off to Paradise in Paradise.

The next morning the sun rose quickly and I took a shower to invigorate my body. Closing my eyes, the water felt so good and every little droplet nourished my dry skin back to life. Then I felt a soft kiss on my back and a strong embrace of breast on my lower back. I turned around and Enaya was in the shower with me gazing in my eyes. I will never forget the images of her Nefertiti type shape, the twinkle in her eyes and the softness of her lips. We kissed and hugged as the water allowed our bodies to embrace and slide across each other with ease. I had to look at Enaya to enjoy her beauty so I gently pushed her back and rubbed my fingers through her flowing hair. Her eyes were closed as I spun her backside to me and pulled her into a loving embrace and kissed her neck. She moaned with pleasure as I walked her out to the bedroom not letting go for one second as my Muslim delight might slip away or change her mind. To my surprise, my eyes flickered in all the candles that Enaya had lit around the room. Our body shadow flickered in the wall like one giant moving mound in the candle lit light. The only thing missing was some Whispers music but I would turn Enaya on to the

Whispers, a 1980s R&B band, later during our trip. Needless to say, we made passionate love and my brain is indented with that moment of love forever. But in the back of my mind and to this day I wondered if my act of love with this Muslim woman was an act that angered God. My entry, no pun intended, to the world of Islam was complicated by the act of love but I have no regrets and I would do it all over again if given the chance. As Enaya and I tired of love making, we fell to the bed and enjoyed the smell of the flickering candles and our images projected on the wall. We said little as not much needed to be said. I loved her dearly and as my woman she loved me. I had rebounded from the deep loveless cavern of my divorce. The question now was could I maintain my personal and spiritual growth through time? Time was not my friend before and it would be a worthy opponent for this time as well.

I bought Enaya an engagement ring on that trip to Singapore. Looking back in retrospect it was clearly premature but at the time it just felt right. It was a nice ring and cost over $7000 in American currency which goes far in the Singapore market for diamonds. I do not think Enaya was impressed by the quality of the diamond as she had an exquisite collection of Indonesian jewelry that had been collected by her from her husband's business dealings. Some of the gifts of jewelry by the large corporations to her were in the hundreds of thousands of dollars. Although my engagement did not impress Enaya materialistically, it did impress upon her my sincere authentic love for her and our union. As I bought the ring Enaya displayed it proudly and said "I can't wait to show Auntie". Auntie was Enaya's paternal Aunt who lived close to her in Jakarta. I had spoken on the phone with Auntie several times and we joked about meeting her in Indonesia. Although I had bought Enaya the ring, I hadn't decided to give it to her to take back to Australia. I had some time to decide as the ring had to be sized for her and I would pick the ring up later during the trip. What the ring did proclaim indirectly was that I would become a Muslim. During the Singapore trip, Enaya and I saw many Muslims seamlessly interact with the Western style culture of Singapore with ease. Enaya reminded that the Indonesian culture was totally different as Indonesia was a thriving Muslim nation with an expanding young demographic. She emphasized the strict observance of Islamic tradition and that our union would be under strict scrutiny in Indonesia and that I would not be able to stay at her house. These small intricate details of my dealing with Enaya reinforced the central core of our union depended upon my conversion to Islam to make Enaya an honest women. After I bought the ring, Enaya and I never discussed my conversion to Islam ever again. I guess we just assumed that this would occur. Enaya even joked we would have a huge party at her house in Australia to celebrate the conversion. Deep in my heart I wanted all these things to happen but in the long term I struggled with my conversion to Islam. I picked up the engagement ring for Enaya and gave it to her over a nice dinner in downtown Singapore. Ironically, I did not drop down on one knee to ask Enaya to marry me. I just remember holding her hand and sliding the beautiful ring on her hand. Enaya beamed with pride with the symbol of our union on her hand. I loved Enaya with all my heart and soul. However, my engagement to her was rushed and I probably did not have adequate downtime from the divorce to make a sound decision. I loved her and did not want to lose her. This marriage seemed right. On the flight back to the USA from Singapore, I had mixed emotions. I felt the high from the physical union of Enaya and me, but I also felt the low from the undecided Islamic conversion necessary for our formal union despite the engagement ring. The next couple of months would decide our fate.

When I got back to the USA, I was optimistic about Enaya and me. We talked every morning as usual and she was still beaming from the engagement ring. Things were kosher for the first three months of the relationship with heightened expectations. In fact, I was pretty shocked myself when I knew that the relationship between us could not continue, as I was not a Muslim nor would I ever be a Muslim. The revelation that I was not a Muslim came on a family visit to the old homestead in Luray, Virginia. I don't know why I started taking a few trips to Luray, but I found the mountains peaceful and it reminded me of the stories that my mother told me about mountain life in 1940s Virginia. I ran into my Uncle Walter and Aunt Cyn when I returned to Luray. I would stop by their house, and they would receive me cordially. We were family as Aunt Cyn was my mother's sister and probably her closest sister. I enjoyed my talks with my Uncle

Walter and he gave me the history of Luray along with the Taylor and Porter Luray history. Uncle Walter told the story of old Luray of proud free Black men that worked in the mountains to avoid the severe racism on the mainland. In the 1940s, the roads to get up the mountain to Luray were very dangerous and many cars fell over the side due to the steep winding roads. This led to a relatively sedentary life for free Black men of Luray and the town was dominated by two Black families at the time. In early Luray, you were either a Taylor or a Porter and the rivalry or competition between the families was intense. My mother was born a Taylor and I remember the pictures she had of the early Taylor family and they did not look Black to me. They looked like Indians and I am pretty sure that the Taylor family had a strong Indian influence. It is well known that Luray, Virginia, had Native American settlements from tribes known as the Sioux, Cherokee, and Iroquois. It is a common belief that the Indians co-mingled with the free Blacks to populate much of the barren mountainside in early Virginia. Uncle Walter told the harsh stories of early Luray and the toughness required to survive the mountain. Uncle Walter sensing the importance of the history to me took me to the Taylor Porter burial grounds where on one side was buried Taylors and on the other side Porters. He took care of the Black cemetery in Virginia formerly known as Blackford Cemetery. I wondered why Uncle Walter took so much time to take care of the old Black cemetery which was no small task and then it hit me like a brick. The mountains of Luray and the valleys of Shenandoah were nothing like the lands of Indonesia or Sydney, Australia. It was almost as if my ancestors were speaking to me and calling out my destiny and heritage. If I left for Indonesia, no matter how good the life, I would forever be disconnected from my heritage and family. This would be a high price to pay for the Indonesian beauty. In addition, I would have to convert to a religion and a culture which was light years removed from the culture of the hard-working men of Luray. The Indians and the free Blacks of Luray did not need Islam to survive the harshest environments and racist societies of America. In their whispering voice at the cemetery, my ancestors called on me to embrace my heritage and to reclaim its perch of honor to the best of my ability. In his own way, Uncle Walter by taking care of the Black cemetery was claiming his heritage and protecting the elders. I respected Uncle Walter for his dedication to the Taylor and Porter clan by protecting those who could not help themselves. With this new found identity, I knew I would have trouble going to a Mosque and trying to convert to Islam. I finally knew the heritage of my soul and it could not comply with a foreign faith. Although Islam is a great religion practiced by billions, it was not for this descendant of Black Cherokee Indians of Luray.

As I drove down the mountain, I fretted about the conversation that I would have with Enaya. She had given me so much and had opened my eyes to a world East of the West with so much potential and opportunity for me. But I had an unclaimed duty to my cultural heritage as I sought to build my future by resurrecting the inner-city urban economy and ultimately a connection to the mountains of Luray. This was a long arduous task but doable with the strong work ethic implanted by generations of Taylors and Porters.

I finally got to a quiet place where I could call Enaya. The timing was reversed from my usual call with her. It was evening in America but morning in Australia. Enaya immediately sensed a difference as she said, "Ken, why the early call? What's wrong?"

I didn't hem or haw. I said, "Enaya, I have something to tell you. I have been struggling with this but I can't convert to Islam. It's just not in me and I'm sorry."

The line went silent for a moment and it kept silent for a while as I heard a whimper.

"Enaya, Enaya, please don't cry."

She finally spoke up, "Oh Ken, that is easy for you to say."

I sensed some anger in her voice which was unexpected but what kind of emotion was the right emotion to the bad news. I kept quiet as I awaited her next reaction. As I waited, the line went silent. Enaya had hung up and that was the last that I ever heard from her. I sat in quiet for a moment as I grasped my conversation with Enaya. I guess Enaya had enough of the long journey with her potential young prince. Ironically, I also was relieved as I had a clear path for my future. A future that did not include Enaya but more importantly a future that did not include Islam.

18

THE QUEEN OF QUEENS

MY EXPERIENCE IN THE HOUSE by myself left me with a frail body and a confused mind after my wife left me. Till this day, I do not know how I found a divorce lawyer and muscled the energy to attend the divorce proceedings. It was an awkward and difficult process. First, it was difficult explaining my physical breakdown to complete strangers, although they were very professional. I finally settled on a female lawyer who was as tough as a Pitbull. She made me feel comfortable, although she was very Southern. But a Southern lawyer was exactly what I needed in the conservative courts of Virginia. Secondly, I barely had the physical strength to attend my lawyer's meetings and finally the divorce. It all came together quickly as the divorce was uncontested and no children were involved. It was as simple as cutting an apple pie in half. I was served divorce papers in June of 2016, and the divorce was final by November of 2016. This was a painful process but I came to grips with it pretty quickly and I actually had more money for myself after the divorce than I had before the divorce. When you pay for mostly 100% of everything, it is a good deal to have your counterpart claim their 50% of the liabilities. I was content and relaxed at the divorce proceedings that it was finally coming to an end. Janet never looked at me nor spoke to me. Probably the most painful part of the divorce process was Janet lying that I hit her. Let me be clear, I never touched Janet or came close to any physical abuse. In fact, during my illness I was probably physically incapable of hitting her, but it was a low blow, and it hurt. I remember reading the divorced papers in shock as it talked of me hitting her. It was really unnecessary as the divorce was uncontested but Janet had a tough attorney and he tried to sway the judge to punish me as an abuser. Thankfully, the judge treated the case as just a division of assets and we moved on. I was finally free of my union to Janet but I now had to confront my ailments internally and externally. I was ready for the fight.

The time period from September 2016 to November 2016 forced me to galvanize my energy and confront the present along with thinking of the future. What was I going to do with my new found freedom? I can remember my lawyer saying in her Southern drawl, "Ken you should be proud of yourself. You pulled yourself up by bootstraps and got it done. Now you can go on with your life."

I looked her in the eye and managed a smile but an empty feeling came over me as I drove home to 12314 Quail Oak Court. The house was big and the silence of the house pierced my ears as I closed the door. Immediately, I wondered whether my future was with my dream house on the 10 acres.

A few weeks went by with me trying to construct a plan of action. Ironically, my daughter's voice rang in my head as she visited one time while I was ill. She was trained in biology and psychology at St. John's University. Kirsten kept reminding me that I needed a plan of action as she repeated, "Daddy what's your plan?"

I did have a plan. I wanted to return home to take care of my mother and start a nonprofit foundation that focused on economic development and finance. As I thought of my plan, my mental confusion slowly went away and my physical strength gradually improved, but I was not out of the woods.

As the New Year approached, I was hopeful of a good 2017. Twenty sixteen had been hell, and I needed a fresh start. After the divorce, I started reaching out to old friends and started to try and reclaim some of my old relationships. It was hard as my guy friends felt I had abandoned them and were very critical of the way I handled my divorce in a secluded manner. It was as if they were mad at me for not contacting them rather than having a true concern for my well-being. The only friend that understood my handling of the divorce was Joe Jordan. Joe had been through divorce and he knew how tough it was to stop the self-pity party. I remember his words exactly to me. Joe said, "Daniels," as he often called me over our 50-year friendship, "These guys are more concerned about their feelings than you and they don't have the capacity to recognize that they are wrong." His words warmed me and gave me hope that things would be alright

On the other hand, my interest in female companionship also grew as I got stronger and stronger. I joined Facebook as an avenue of reconnecting socially, and I was amazed to find a lot of old friends readily available. I found one Fairfield University friend, Dawn, who was very active on Facebook as a community leader. I was hesitant to contact Dawn but I reached out to say hello. Dawn and I had taken classes together at Fairfield University and respected each other intellectually. Dawn responded immediately and was aware of my divorce. She recognized that I was looking for friends. We talked briefly about our college days before I asked, "How is your good friend, 0?"

Dawn hesitated and said, "She's good. She is single and living in Queens."

Felisha was my first love at Fairfield University as we dated when she was a senior and I was a freshman. I was smitten with Felisha and had strong feelings for her that probably swamped the puppy love that I felt in high school. I knew that Felisha felt the same way about me without a doubt. She mysteriously disappeared after her graduation, and I had not seen her in over 40 years. Was she still the pretty and intoxicating beauty from Queens or had time been harsh to her? I wanted to find out. Without reservation, I asked Dawn could I have Felisha's phone number. Dawn hesitated again.

She said, "Let me check with Felisha and see if it is okay." I was disappointed but I respected Dawn's wisdom on the matter.

A few days went by and I had not heard from Dawn, when unexpectedly I got a Facebook message from her. The message read, "Here is Felisha's number and why do not you call her."

I felt good that Dawn had gotten consent from Felisha, and she wanted to hear from me or so I thought. Later, I learned that Dawn did me a favor and trusted me with her friend.

With Felisha's number in hand, I started to ponder on how to reach out to her. What do I say? I had been a total recluse for over a year and I still was not very comfortable venturing out the house. Was I ready for a relationship? No, I wasn't ready for a relationship but I needed a friend. Most of my guy friends had bailed on me and although Joe understood my plight, he was not the warm and fuzzy type. I needed a friend and companion to help me get back to normal.

After much thought I decided to trust my instincts when calling Felisha. I once loved this woman even before Janet. I was hopeful that her curiosity would match mine, and we would rediscover our friendship.

With confidence in my game plan, I gave Felisha a call. The phone rang and rang with no answer on the first try. The second day, I called again in the evening as it got dark in the house. I was lonely again in the house, and I desperately wanted Felisha to pick up the phone and say hello in a sexy voice. To no avail again, the phone rang and rang with no answer. This continued for two weeks. With persistence, I followed my emotions and called my past lover diligently every night hoping for a response. About the third week, I was ready to give up, because clearly Felisha did not want to speak with me. Again, maybe my fairytale romance was one-sided and only authentic for me. Had I misgauged our love and made a mistake by calling? With hesitation, I placed a final call, and I was surprised when I heard a hello in a mild, soft, silky voice. My Felisha picked up the phone.

I said, "Hello, Felisha. This is Ken Daniels from Fairfield."

She quickly responded, "I know it's you Daniels. Dawn told me she gave you my number."

As I heard her response, I was relieved and anxious at the same time. I was excited that she picked up the phone, but I sensed some reluctance on her part. I interjected to try and resolve her uncertainty.

I said, "Well, I am glad you picked up the phone. All my life I have thought about you. You have never left my mind."

Felisha was from Queens and was tough as nails but as soft as butter. If you could wrestle this combination you would be dealt one helluva sensual sexy ride. Simply put, Felisha was pure pleasure and raw emotions.

She chimed right back at me, "Well Daniels, I never forgot about you either and that's why I was afraid to answer the phone." She continued, " I told Dawn I was pissed that she gave you my number."

Not knowing where Felisha was going with the conversation, I butted in, "Why didn't you contact me before you left Fairfield?"

A long silence fell over the phone. She finally responded, "You were young and innocent while I was hungry to start my career. I was never going to come back to Fairfield and being with you would have just made it hard."

Felisha and I talked for hours. Our conversation shifted to laughter and fun as we talked about the good old days. By the stroke of luck, I found my friend, my companion in the Queen of Queens. She would turn out to be the exact opposite of Janet. She was loyal to a fault as she learned of my ailments and she aided my recovery. In retrospect she probably saved my life as she pumped sensuality, pleasure, and energy through the window of my soul to awaken the sleeping carcass of a Black man back to reality.

I wanted to get with Felisha so bad that I traveled to New York a couple of times to see her. She lived in a multicultural section of Queens with a heavy Hispanic and Asian population. Her building, which was primarily Black, was a nice coop that was well taken care of and named after Dorie Miller, a Black sailor who was a war hero. It was the first federally funded housing project in Queens, New York for Blacks. Although the federal government funded Levittown and other housing projects in New York, Blacks were segregated away from the White population and not allowed to buy housing in Levittown during its construction. This was an obvious abuse of the federal government's purchasing power and blatantly discriminatory. The effects of these policies are still impacting Black people in 2020.

Felisha worked a difficult nine to five job but was amazing in her dedication to see me get back to 100%. After my initial visits to Queens in early 2017, I would never visit again in any frequent fashion over the summer of 2017. Over the summer of 2017, I had a partial relapse as the indecisiveness of my work plan coupled with the loneliness of the work week caught up to me. Felisha in heroic fashion drove from Queens to Ashland, Virginia, every weekend to attend to literally my every need. God had sent an unwavering angel to save me. Without a doubt, I needed help in my recovery and the Queen of Queens came through. I often wonder what would have happened to me if Felisha did not answer that phone call. Only God knows, but clearly Felisha helped me avoid a disaster.

After the summer of 2017, with the help of Felisha, I fully recovered to get on my feet and miraculously start working again. By November of 2017, I was well enough to take Felisha on a trip to Myrtle Beach, and we had a fabulous time. I still remember her face as she walked onto the plane. She looked marvelous, and she was mine. Felisha's name means happiness, and she charms every soul she meets with unadulterated kindness and respect. The flight to Myrtle Beach was a short flight. I could not stand being away from Felisha as she sat in the front row. We finally landed, and we walked off the plane together. She grabbed me around the waist with her fully embracing smile, and we fell in love again for a second time. I will never forget that week in Myrtle Beach. Felisha gave of herself freely and to my surprise my body responded automatically to her wishes. I was back physically to my old self and had ridded myself of the low testosterone syndrome. I wish I could write a fairytale ending but just as much pleasure as Felisha gave, she could take back with some inner demons that possessed her body on occasion. Go figure, it would be my luck that as soon as I got divorced that I would run into a woman that has some spiritual deficiencies. Little did I know how deep these spiritual deficiencies would run.

To be frank, I thought Felisha was playing when she first told me she was a witch. Who in their right mind actually believes that they have power not of this earth? After the divorce, I eventually moved in with Felisha in her Queens coop. It was a perfect transition for me as I was close to my mother, and home which gave me a purpose. Although Felisha's coop was in good condition, her apartment needed work as she was a single parent, and her twenty-four-year-old daughter lived with her. It was an awkward arrangement at first, but they both accepted me willingly. I was home most of the day by myself as Felisha went to work and her daughter went to school. Initially, I stayed in the house pretty much, but then I started to discover New York, and it was a fun place to live. This is when Felisha's behavior started to change towards me.

Things were going great between Felisha and I. With my new found money and furniture from Virginia, I helped her refurbish her apartment into a modern living arrangement. I was even building a relationship with her daughter, and then one day, Felisha snapped. As I mentioned I started to explore New York, every day I got up and explored the rich multicultural neighborhoods. Felisha didn't like this, and on this day, she said in a jealous manner, "So are you going to walk the streets again today to find some find Spanish whore?"

My jaw pretty much dropped to the floor in shock as she had never talked to me in a derogatory manner up to this time. Responding to her accusations, I said, "What makes you think I am out looking for whores?"

Felisha did not answer me but just got dressed and left. I kept my routine as I went out for coffee, and on this day, I took the trains to New Jersey to visit my mom. I was gone a full day and got home late as the trip by train from East Orange, New Jersey, was a long ride.

As I opened the door to the apartment, I saw Felisha and her daughter burning incense. I did not think much of their chanting and smoke until I saw the doll. Alarmed at their actions, I asked, "What are you two doing?"

Very casually Felisha answered, "We are cleansing your spirit by tongue."

Immediately I thought in my mind, these bitches were crazy as the daughter gleefully smiled at me. My thought process immediately shifted to the conversation where Felisha told me she had powers and was a witch.

Confronting Felisha directly I said, "Come on Felisha, stop this nonsense."

She seemed startled that I approached her and she screamed, "No! We are going to stop you from fucking these whores."

I was now livid and I said, "That's enough!"

I chased Felisha back towards the front door and locked her out of the apartment. Felisha was now locked outside but when I turned around her daughter quickly walked up on me and spit right in my face. Shocked at what just happened, I just stared at the daughter in disbelief.

The daughter then looked me squarely in the eyes and said, "I am a witch also and if you aren't careful, I will put a spell on you."

She then walked past me and let her mother back in the house. Looking at the two witches, I stared in disbelief and walked to the bathroom to clean my face. Not wanting anymore confrontation with literally nowhere to go, I walked into our bedroom and closed the door. Sitting down watching television the night slipped away and Felisha slept on the couch. The next morning, she got up and dressed for work like nothing happened. She was cordial with me and even made me breakfast before she left. The daughter, on the other hand, peered at me cautiously in a threatening manner as she left for class without mentioning a word. As I sat in the apartment by myself, I knew I had to get out of the relationship with Felisha. I wanted to leave but I felt obliged to stay with the woman who had shown me so much loyalty. Was it right to leave the relationship after this awful event?

I knew the answer but the act of leaving became more complicated as time went on, and Felisha threatened to hurt herself if I left. I stayed for a good while after that but eventually the arguments between Felisha and I became more frequent and the unfounded jealous taunts became louder and more violent. I eventually left to stay with my mother in New Jersey after Felisha locked me out of the apartment one night after a jealousy-ridden fight. I was again confused and bewildered as I moved in with my mother. I had my freedom, but I was back living at my childhood home and sleeping on the couch. My relationship with Felisha was over in my mind, but little did I know how difficult it would be to displace her spell on me.

19

THE KIDNAPPING

A SON'S LOVE FOR HIS MOTHER is almost immeasurable and it goes deep. I loved my mom in so many ways and the memories of her at different stages of my life were vivid. These memories of my mother kept me focused, kept me balanced, and happy about my immediate family life. I had memories of me as a kid using my mom as a mountain as I rolled the play trucks up and over her sleeping beauty. I was always by her side and we did a lot together. One activity that we always did together when I was a child was plant flowers together in the backyard of the house at 100 Park End Place. 100 is what I called it. The garden at 100 represented a happy time in my life and a special relationship with my mom. The garden represented our nurturing relationship and it represented growth. I think one of the reasons I cultivated a garden in Virginia was to try to reach back to my mom and extend our nurturing relationship through my garden.

I came back to 100 to help take care of my mom after my illness and after living in New York for a period. When I first came back to 100, I was surprised to learn that a lot of different people were living in the house with my mom that were not family members. I expected Theresa to be living at

100. Theresa was the sister of my sister-in-law Linda who was married to my brother Keith. Theresa was a nurse, and she was the primary caregiver of my mother who was 89 years old in 2016. Thelma adored my mom and initially gave my mom adequate care. However, Theresa had a full-time nursing job while taking care of my mom, and as I observed her care-giving, I saw that the care being given to my mom was not adequate. In reality, no one was taking care of my mom as everyone was too busy with their own responsibilities and life. For example, Theresa would get up and give my mother breakfast and leave the house for work. She would then return home for lunch and rush to give my mom lunch, usually just a sandwich, and leave for work again. Theresa would then return to give my mom dinner and then leave the house. In the interim, Cindy, the daughter of my mom's best friend, who had died, also lived in the house. Cindy was supposed to come down stairs after Theresa left and read bible verses to my mother. This never occurred as Cindy would get up and leave the house. Cindy had gone through emotional abuse in her life and was a troubled person while living in the house as she had psychiatric problems. She lived in one of the upstairs bedrooms. When I entered her bedroom one day to check on it, I found a filthy room with garbage and clothes strewn all over the room in an unacceptable unsanitary manner. Cindy had the approval of my mother to stay in the house, and my mother cared about her well-being. However, Cindy was not performing her responsibilities in the house that was arranged by my brother Kevin, the twin of Keith. Also living in the house currently was Theresa's son with his young son and Miles the son of Pickle in the basement.

Miles was another person who had past problems. In general, the house was not well kept as the rugs were dirty and the kitchen was not clean. My brothers had arranged for these individuals to take care of my mom and the house but neither was being done in a satisfactory manner. Probably the most troubling care of my mom was her hygiene and her bathing. My mom had fallen the previous year and had broken her hip. She could no longer climb the stairs at 100 which were steep and a two-tier staircase. My mom slept downstairs on a small bed in the den but all the bathrooms in the house were upstairs. As I observed the care of my mom over a month's period, she never went upstairs to the bathrooms to take a bath. She could not climb the stairs to be washed so Theresa or Cindy were supposed to bathe her in her room. This rarely occurred and when you entered my mom's bedroom in the small den, the stench of the piss was so thick that I almost vomited. My mom used a porta potty and it was always filled with piss and its odor also permeated the room. To make a long story short, I had to improve my mom's living conditions.

I was appalled at the living conditions of my mom at 100, and I had to do something. However, to make sure I was not overreacting, I asked a family friend to come observe the situation. I asked Shivaugn who was a family friend from Union Baptist Church to take a look and she obliged. Upon her review she said to me, "Ken, that is your mother and you have to do something."

I had the confirmation that I needed to act to help my mother. My brothers had set up an absentee owner system to take care of my mother's needs. Kevin lived in Virginia, and Keith in Georgia, and they never or rarely visited 100 to check on my mom. At least they did not visit my mom during my return from New York, in 2016. More importantly, they had an overconfident sense that my mom's assisted living care was acceptable and working properly. I had direct observations that it was not working properly and an independent assessment that something needed to be done to improve the assisted living care of my mother.

I initially was sleeping on the couch when I returned home to live at 100. Every day, I would watch the caregivers carefully and assess the conditions of the house. After I determined that the living conditions were unacceptable, in an attempt to improve the living conditions, I first asked that everyone clean their area and keep the kitchen clean. Then I asked them to vacuum the rugs when they had a chance as the rugs were filthy. I did not ask them to do anything about the care of my mom as I knew this would be a sensitive area. One morning I woke to some loud conversation in my mom's room.

"I told you to eat and get dressed! Didn't you hear me?"

It was Cindy screaming at my mom in an abusive manner. I got up and asked Cindy what was wrong. She said my mom would not eat. That was the last straw that made me spring into action. I immediately told Cindy to not to speak or address my mom in that demeaning and disrespectful manner. Cindy insisted that she was only giving instructions. I told Cindy to leave my mom and that I would feed her. Cindy left the house and went to work.

After the incident with Cindy, I knew I had to accelerate my mom's caregiver plans. I called my brothers to tell them my intentions. I told them I wanted to fix the house and put a bathroom downstairs for our mother. I also wanted to get her a private nurse and fix the rest of the house so it was acceptable for my mom to stay there. I thought my brothers would be okay with my plan. I did not ask them for any money, and I was physically at the house so I thought they would view that favorably. I was wrong in my assessment as they immediately accused me of being selfish and only caring about the house. I was dumbfounded as how could they not want their mother to have an improved house and a private nurse. Our discussions came to head when they said, "If you mess up the arrangements we have for mom, then you are on your own."

I said, "Fine!"

I was prepared to fix the situation with my own time and money. I did not need my brothers, and I was prepared to ask the current caregivers to step up and do their responsibilities appropriately. I started my plan by interviewing private nurses for my mom. I asked around and found the names of several good private nurses in the area for about $125 a week to give proper and professional care for my mom. I finally settled on a Jamaican woman named Portia who had just been let go from a long-term assisted living job. She was experienced and would tidy up the house. This was a perfect solution for the absentee care my mother was presently receiving. Thelma did not approve of my decision to use Portia and informed me that she was moving to Pennsylvania. I did not kick Thelma out of the house, as accused, as she had a new boyfriend in Pennsylvania. She moved there shortly after I began working on the house. Next, I ripped up the filthy rugged that was filled with years of dirt and grime. The hardwood floors beamed underneath but needed repair. If I was going to live in the house with mom, the house needed an overhaul. I went to mom and asked her, "Mom, do you want to stay here and do you want me to fix the house?"

She replied, "Yes Kenneth, fix it. I don't want to go to another home."

I had my marching orders and I began to plan the bathroom downstairs and fix the bathrooms upstairs as they were filthy but worked. I found a contractor easy and we began the work. Initially, I moved mom upstairs as the contractors started to build out the new downstairs bathroom. Portia moved upstairs with mom and mom's upstairs bathroom had running water and the toilet worked. This solution worked for the short term on the renovation but long term I needed to get mom out of the house for the renovation. I asked my brothers could mom come stay with them until the work on the house was done. Kevin replied, "No. You broke what we had and now you are on your own."

I was not deterred and kept on with my plan. I had some timeshare points to use so I planned a two-week trip for Mom and me to go on the road as we needed to evacuate the house. Mom was excited to travel, and she responded positively to being on the road. We went to Massachusetts, the Poconos, and we stayed in first-rate condos. I checked on the house while we were gone and progress was being made.

Things were going well. Mom was bonding with Portia and her care was top notch. I was getting familiar with my new surroundings and the house was almost finished. Unfortunately, I had some unfinished business trips that needed to be attended to before the end of the year in 2016. I had a dilemma on my hands as I could not leave Mom alone and Kevin had declared that he would not help. Reluctantly, I called Kevin one last time and asked him would he look after Mom while I went on my trip to Vancouver. Initially he rejected my request, but then called me back to say that he would watch Mom while I was gone. I was relieved as Mom had proper care now from Portia and Kevin during my absence. Portia was the main caregiver and Kevin just had to oversee Portia during the day and get her home at the end of the day.

I set off to Vancouver on October 5th, 2016, with ambitions of buying some real estate in British Columbia for my foundation. As you might expect, I was excited about the opportunity as I had set out an ambitious game plan for the Daniels Foundation for Impact Investments and Development, which was my post-retirement plan in action. I landed in

Vancouver as expected and almost immediately, I received a phone call from Portia, my mother's caregiver. Portia was speaking frantically on the phone as she said, "Mr. Daniels, your brother took your mother, and he told me I was no longer needed."

Hearing Portia talk of her dismissal and the taking of my mother just did not make sense to me. I tried to process the situation Portia was describing and calm her at the same time. I said to Portia, "Don't worry Portia. You still have a job. Don't worry about your job or pay. I will see you when I get back."

Immediately, I had a crisis on my hands as my mother was practically kidnapped from my care and taken by my brother to Virginia initially. In addition, I had a formal financial obligation to Portia as her employer that I had to digest. In Vancouver, I continued my business as quickly as possible but as you might imagine, I was not able to take my time and conduct business as usual. I finished up things in Vancouver, flew back to Newark, and arrived back home in East Orange on a Sunday. The flight from west coast to east coast is grueling and I got some rest in 100 as I prepared to deal with the crisis my brother, Kevin, had created. Almost immediately, I sensed the reality of the situation as the house was barren without my mother's presence. All my hard work showed in the physical reconstruction of the house as the bedroom downstairs now had a completed bath. The kitchen had been completely renovated as the wall had been taken out to make a seamless transition between the kitchen and the dining room. I had waited for the opportunity to share all these changes with my mom but now all that would have to wait. The physical changes to the house meant nothing without my mother. Why would I go through all these changes, especially a bedroom and bath downstairs, without my mother to enjoy these benefits?

The absurd new reality set it and I called Kevin to ask his rationale for taking our mother. I had actually called Kevin from Vancouver, but I got no response. As I called Kevin from the house in New Jersey, his phone just rang and rang. Clearly, Kevin was not answering the phone and this behavior went on for about 10 days or close to two weeks. I was now frantic as I was concerned about my mother's physical well-being as she did not have access to her medication. I called several friends describing the situation and they could not believe the circumstances. One of my friends suggested a wellness check with the Virginia Beach police department as my brother resided in Virginia Beach. Not having many options, I called the Virginia Beach police department. They asked the pertinent things such as name, age, and physical location of my mother along with my relationship to her.

I learned a lot about guardianship nuances during this time as the wellness check did not give me any right but was done solely to assess the physical well-being of my mother. I received a return phone call from the Virginia Beach police department informing me that my mother was at the Virginia Beach location of my brother, Kevin, and that she was physically okay. This was the extent of the Virginia Beach police department's responsibility to me.

After my initial attempt to contact my brother and the wellness check, I tried to reach my brother, Kevin, through some of his friends. One of his friends, Fields, was receptive to helping as he had been a childhood friend that lived on the same street as 100 but in the middle of the block. Fields and his sister, Karen, were close to our family and you could almost consider them extended family as we grew up in a close-knit community in 1960s urban East Orange. I remember telling Fields how I was taking care of Mom and that Kevin came to watch her while I was on a business trip. I then proceeded to tell him that Kevin had taken my mom and was failing to return my phone calls. Fields sensing the alarm in my voice said "Ken, I'm sorry."

Even though Fields had empathy for my plight with my mother, he was on a business trip and could not immediately help. Fields indicated that he would talk to his sister Karen and see if she would contact Kevin as they had a long history together as childhood friends. I was relieved that someone was taking an interest and Fields implied that Karen would be in touch. I knew Karen but not as well as Fields so I didn't know what to expect.

A few days went by and then just as Fields mentioned, Karen gave me a phone call. We had not spoken or seen each other in over 40 years. It is amazing how although many years had passed, I still recognized the strength of Karen's voice and visualized her face. Karen and I exchanged pleasantries and then we started discussing my problem. Karen indicated she had spoken to Fields and wanted to help because she knew our family well. Again, I felt relief. Karen asked me to explain what happened, then she said, "Ken, I will do my best to contact your brother, but I don't know if he will be receptive as I haven't spoken to Kevin in years."

I understood Karen's reservation as no one had heard from Kevin or Keith for that matter. As my cell phone conversation with Karen ended, I started a waiting game to hear a response on the welfare of my mother. A week passed and I became increasingly concerned as I did not know my mother's whereabouts. Finally, one evening I received a phone call from Karen. I remember the phone call particularly as I was very emotional and I got into an emotional debate with Karen for which I am still sorry for till this day.

Karen began the conversation with, "Ken, I talked to your brother and he is very upset with you."

As you might expect, I was confused as to why my brother would be upset. Karen continued, "I spoke to your brother at length and he told me to tell you that he is not bringing your mother back home. Also, you will never see your mother again."

As Karen indicated the finality of me not seeing my mom, an anger gripped my body and I let out an emotional cry to Karen. I said, "Karen, how can my brother not let me not see my mother? What did he say that I did?"

Karen politely told me that her conversation with my brother was confidential and that she would not discuss their conversation with me. All sudden I rightly or wrongly felt a double slight as Karen was protecting my emotional assailant. I forcibly asked Karen, "How can you support such behavior?"

Karen fired right back at me, "Ken, I have a right to handle this matter as I see fit and I am acting as an intermediary out of respect for the family."

Immediately, I knew I had gone too far with my emotional fit and put Karen in an uncomfortable position. Karen and I ended our conversation with agreeing to disagree. Given the finality of my brother's word without any just cause left me with an empty feeling. It also put me in a disadvantageous position as I had to now come to grips that I could not speak to my mother, my number one confidant. I really did not know what to do as I went to sleep that night all alone in the house that I had renovated for my mother.

A few days went by and I pondered my course of action by talking to several people regarding my guardianship problem with my mother. Then one day, Fields called after returning from his business trip. I answered Fields's call and immediately he said with bass in his voice, "Ken, you're cut off."

I asked Fields courteously, "Fields, what's wrong? What happened?"

Again, with bass in his voice, Fields said, "You went off on Karen."

Everything now made sense as my emotional conversation with Karen had provoked a brotherly response. I said to Fields, "Fields, Karen and I had a very emotional conversation where we both said some spirited things about a difficult situation."

In the back of my mind, I knew I had come close to the line of insulting Karen, but Karen was a strong-willed Black woman physically, as she was a bodybuilder, and mentally. Karen was no shrinking violet and did not need her brother's protection. Fields came back to me, "Ken, you are cut-off now from all my contacts." I was stunned as I had helped Fields get access to the VCU School of Engineering before I left VCU. Ending our conversation, I said, "Fields, your contacts have never come through for me so there is nothing to cut off."

As we ended our confrontation, I told Fields that I apologized for any perceived insult to Karen and I hope she accepted my apology. I sunk into my living room couch bewildered at the turn of events. I had shattered two childhood friendships as a result of my brother's kidnapping of my mother and the emotional damage was picking up steam as it went unchecked. To this day as of the writing of this chapter, November 2020, I am not allowed to see my mom and my brother Keith gives me a very hard time scheduling the once in a while Zoom meetings. This psychological warfare has gone on since my brother kidnapped my mother in 2016. I have not allowed this behavior to bother me and believe God will hold my brother's accountable. My mother knows I love her, and I am at peace.

20

A ROCKY ROAD HOME

I HAD HIGH EXPECTATIONS, personally and professionally, coming back home. I truly believed and I still believe that my injection into an urban East Orange, New Jersey, was not by chance but a direct action of God. Things started off badly as my brothers kidnapped my mother and left me with a deep void to fill. I used the void to focus primarily on the development of my foundation, The Daniels Foundation for Impact Investments and Development.

The idea for the foundation stemmed from my board workdays in Virginia, and in particular, my work on the bank board of VCC. VCC is a leader in the social capital movement and not much work has been done at the grassroots level in urban neighborhoods with significant resources. I viewed the foundation as a capital raising vehicle to fuel financial assets into risky neighborhoods with less risk involved in the process. The foundation would invest in hard assets but also try to improve the human capital of the inner-city core through training in basic fundamentals such as technology, financial literacy, and the arts.

The foundation got off to a good start with the development of its website and the donation of a few computers to the Toussaint Louverture Elementary School. Ralph Jacobs was the principal of the school and a childhood friend. Ralph took the challenged elementary school, which bordered several poor neighborhoods, and instilled discipline and pride in the school and its students. Ralph asked me to give the keynote address at the school graduation, and I marshalled enough energy to give an adequate address but nowhere near the legendary sermons my father would give as principal of the old Columbian School.

One reason to look at the Columbian School project is that it illustrated the massive migration of White flight from the City of East Orange. Columbian School derived its name from the fact that it opened in the 400th year after the discovery of America by Columbus. Originally, it was an eight-room building and was considered one of the most complete schools in the state of New Jersey on its opening. It was built at the corner of Springdale Avenue and Grove Street and just 100 pupils occupied its spacious quarters on opening. Good schools and affordable housing made East Orange an attractive draw for aspiring Whites, and the city grew significantly in the roaring 1920s. This spaciousness didn't last long. As the population in the Fifth Ward of East Orange began increasing by leaps and bounds, the 7th and 8th grades had to be transferred. Before the renovation, Columbian School had 35 classrooms, two gyms, many special classrooms and a teaching staff of 46 members. It housed over 1,000 students. Between 1950 and 1970, East Orange went through a massive migration of Blacks to the inner cities and Whites to the suburbs. Columbian School is an interesting symbol of this urban change. My father was the past principal of Columbian School, the well-known elementary school on a busy economic corridor near the border of Newark. My father took over Columbian School as a turnaround project in the early 1960s as the drugs and gangs from Newark made the surrounding Rutledge neighborhood a gritty neighbor with an abundant housing supply.

The housing supply of the Rutledge neighborhood had been built during the heydays of East Orange, and its Presidential district was declared a national historic district. The current Rutledge neighborhood had seen better days and was in need of significant investment to reclaim its heyday status.

The City of East Orange recognized the importance of the neighborhood and invested $41.2 million in a new elementary school that was built on the original site and bordered the old Columbian Park. The new 77,000 square-foot Sheila Y. Oliver Elementary School will provide the East Orange School District with space to educate a maximum of approximately 500 students in Pre-Kindergarten to 5th grade. The school includes 24 general classrooms, two self-contained special education classrooms, a science lab, a cafeteria, multi-purpose room with stage, a media center, a music room, an art room, a technology lab, and necessary support spaces.

I thought the school was a great opportunity to launch a full-blown economic development of the Rutledge corridor. Sensing an opportunity, I wrote a complete economic development plan to the East Orange School Board. First, I outlined a project that would rename the school after my father to honor his noteworthy dedication and years of service to Columbian School and the surrounding neighborhood. Second, the foundation proposed a series of curriculum enhancing programs such as financial literacy to aid the development of the students. Lastly, the foundation put forward a plan to develop the blighted housing and lots of the nearby Rutledge neighborhood as affordable housing for potential parents and students. See the site plans at the end of the book as concrete evidence. The proposal was submitted under the guidelines established by the East Orange Board of Education which specifically mentions that a new school cannot be named after a standing politician.

After submitting my application, I waited and waited, and I heard nothing of my submission. By chance, I met an East Orange Board of Education board member at the East Orange Hall of Fame induction ceremony. Her name was Cathy Howard, and I told her of my plans. Ms. Howard was polite and quiet and listened to me but was obviously distracted by the Hall of Fame events. Rushing me off like a school child she said, "Just email me your proposal," while handing me her business card, "and I'll make sure the Board takes a look."

I felt pretty good as I had followed the rules and a sitting board member was willing to hand my proposal personally to the Board.

Little did I know that this was the usual run-around in doing business in East Orange. If you did not know someone of economic or political power, then you were subjected to rudimentary treatment that did not suit your means. This was very ironic as I knew the mayor and several key people in power in the city.

In this case, it didn't matter as the power structure was hell-bent on naming the school after the sitting lieutenant governor of the State of New Jersey, Sheila Oliver. According to the State of New Jersey website, Lieutenant Governor Oliver is a self-described "Jersey Girl," born and raised in an ethnically diverse Newark neighborhood. Lieutenant Governor Oliver was inspired as a young girl to be a fighter for the voiceless when her eyes were opened to societal injustices and inequalities around her, often citing "A Tale of Two Cities" as her youth awakening.

She has since pioneered a successful career in public service advocating for social justice, women's equality, and education, ultimately becoming the first woman of color to serve in a statewide elected office in New Jersey history. While Ms. Oliver may have been a good aspirational candidate for the school renaming, she did not pour blood and sweat into reshaping the Columbian School legacy and transforming the nearby neighborhoods. Plus, as I mentioned, the School Board Policy explicitly stated that a school could not be named after a politician. Clearly, the East Orange School Board was not going to violate their own policy.

Boy was I wrong. Not only was the School Board going to violate its own policy, the School Board was going to ignore the history of the neighborhood and not take full advantage of the current opportunity. Remember, I had submitted an extensive economic development plan for the neighborhood along with the renaming of the elementary school. What was more troubling was the misrepresentation of the issue by the school board to the community.

I attended a School Board meeting where the school renaming project was on the docket for discussion. Ironically, a few community members were very astute of the school renaming project problems and illustrated them clearly to the board. Without any respect for the community, the school board held a minor discussion and passed the motion to rename the new Columbian School in the honor of Sheila Oliver. Everyone in the room was disgusted. I observed the process from the back of the room and an ill feeling fell over my stomach. I felt I had let down my Dad because he was deserving of the honor, but more importantly, the community did not get the best options for their future.

I was so convinced that I was on the right side of justice that I hired a Virginia attorney to pursue the case against the East Orange School Board. In fact, I hired two attorneys to investigate the case and make a claim. The first was David Faux, a well-respected attorney out of New York and Mr. Faux communicated directly with the office of Sheila Oliver to discuss the serious School Board violations and the New Jersey newspaper ran several articles documenting the serious denigration of the East Orange citizenry by the local politicians.

When a citizenry is disrespected and violated so much that they choose silence rather than engagement, then we have lost the case to be considered honorable. It is a shame that the disgusting politics of New Jersey has shamed the people of East Orange into submission and it is even more repulsive that respectable newspapers like the Star Ledger and the legal authorities of the New Jersey FBI, and County attorney's do not confront the obvious abuse of power which is a sinful state of mind and stance given their responsibility to the citizenry and public discourse. The second attorney I hired was Wyatt Durrette out of Virginia from the firm Durrette, Arkema, Gerson and Gill. I was referred to Mr. Durrette by a friend of Greg Schnitzler and we immediately found some common ground of honor and sought to seek justice for my father.

Clearly, the East Orange School Board was wrong and vile in their actions of civic responsibility. In some respect a light is needed to shine on the vile actions of these local leaders as they are slowly bleeding the communities they serve into a slow death and a death by a thousand cuts. You also have to view their actions as systemic racism as they are more likely to attempt this vile behavior in communities of color rather than in communities of European descent.

It is not by accident that every time to "cross the tracks" in every community across the nation that the properties and the people seemed to have lost hope in their communities. Many Black communities have died at the hand of the thousand cuts delivered by incompetent School Boards and local leaders such they dare not act as an engaged citizenry and suffer the disrespectful torture as delivered by the East Orange School Board to me and my father. I blame politicians such as Sheila Oliver for accepting an undeserved as she participates in a fraudulent system and receives a fraudulent benefit. Mr. Durrette, and I fought the good fight but didn't win because New Jersey has a statute stating that any claim against a School Board must be filed within ninety days.

I still disagree with my attorney's assessment and the assessment that we got from a New Jersey attorney, Jennifer Borek. We hired Ms. Borek to research the validity of our claim against the East Orange School Board and even she agreed they had violated their policy and New Jersey law but had the time period expired? Well, I was less than thrilled with Ms. Borek as her law firm, Genova Burns LLC, represented or had ties to the Democratic Committee of New Jersey. We had Ms. Borek initiate discussions with her law partner and the Democratic Committee but the law firm didn't have the common decency to give us a simple response and just blew us off.

In addition, lawyers like Ms. Borek have no incentive to fight the good fight as they are beholden to the profit motive and their career aspirations. This shows the weakness of the law profession as they take no oath to hold themselves to the highest standards that improve the lot of mankind. They do use maximum effort to get paid at all cost and always represent their interest even willing to sacrifice client interest and general community well-being for their benefit. It is one profession where honor is lacking and the disgusting business practices are commonplace such that exorbitant profits can support lavish lifestyles at huge cost to the common decency of mankind.

To make a long story short I had spent over $5,000 to defend my father's legacy and honor with no result. I know some will view this as a useless expenditure but I vehemently disagree as the establishment in NJ and elsewhere must be held accountable and hopefully the responsible parties such as the newspapers and the legal authorities will get wind of these disgusting practices and behavior as the word spreads of their cowardice. I refuse to join in their cowardly behavior and directly blame them along with the political machinery behavior of New Jersey for a declining citizenry involvement.

As of this writing I have given up the fight but am I hopeful that someone will read this story and want to join the good fight with me. It is necessary that we fight the good fights even though we may not succeed to keep the powers that control our society accountable for their actions and I have no regret for taking on the School Board of East Orange.

21

A FINAL PERSPECTIVE

IF I WERE TO DIE TODAY, I would not have one regret. I have lived an incredible life, and I have come a long way on meager resources. In my heart and mind, I know I could have accomplished more professionally. The roadblocks I encountered by individuals such as Dean Ed Grier were unfortunate circumstances that I could not control. Some Black men such as Ed Grier have carried heavy burdens and done some good along with some not so good decisions. In fact, many men like Ed Grier do not have the foresight to recognize their Blackness as a strength and not a weakness. This was a very unfortunate experience for me. I hope Dean Grier can find some peace in the final days of his career, as many had high hopes for him. The final take-away is that Dean Grier is a symbol of the complexity of racism against Black Americans. Black Americans sometimes look the other way to not see racism or they are complicit in the crime of racism. This complexity makes the problem very difficult to provide comprehensive solutions. In hindsight, the roadblocks I encountered actually have steered me to my final destiny and my ultimate contribution which is the Daniels Foundation for Impact Investments and Development. God forced me to leave a lucrative professional career and focus on redirecting my talents to help my people. I am convinced of this and the premonitions and visions that I received of the Promised Land for Black people can only come with some personal sacrifice by the current generation for future generations. When I ride around Northern New Jersey, I see the infrastructure put in by the "Greatest Generation" as labeled by Tom Brokaw, and it was their investment in the next generation which propelled America into an optimistic future. It is with this same optimism that I share the Daniels Foundation with the hope it will garner enough resources and discussion to propel Black Americans to a prosperous future. African American philosophers like Obery Hendricks, Cornel West and Michael Dyson provide very good analysis of the state of Black America and the moral dilemma we face as a people and a nation. However, their commentary always falls short of offering an applied solution or an actual institutional pathway to a better standard of living. In this context, this memoir offers a more detailed approach at offering a vision and a solution for a better way of life. In the long run I hope it provokes some dialogue about institution building in the African American community other than building churches by philanthropic means or government intervention.

Personally, I have some hopes for my family and children. I hope to reconcile with my brothers as I have forgiven them for all their transgressions and hold no ill will towards them. I don't even seek an apology as I am so far removed from any of the pain caused by their actions that an apology really means nothing to my state of mind or feelings. For all their faults, I love my brothers and wish them nothing but happiness and success. As for my children, I hold the same hope of reconciliation. Their acts have hurt me deeply and cut a deep cavern of pain that may never go away. To this day, I don't understand their actions or why they hold deep animosity towards me, their father. In my heart, I know I did the best I knew how to as their Dad. I interacted personally all through their development and I will cherish our memories. I hope that one day they will understand and desire to have a relationship with their father.

At this time, communication is non-existent between us. The cussing out by my daughter and the passive aggressive controlled behavior by my son are unthinkable acts that I would not display to my parents. Although I had many disagreements with my parents, it never crossed my mind to visibly display any act of disrespect or any act to disassociate or dishonor. I have experienced all three with my children. It has been a true pleasure to share some of my adventures, struggles, and hopes with you. I have grown immeasurably over the course of this activity, and I have enjoyed my experience as a writer and hope to continue my profession as a writer and advocate. The final message I would like to express with vigor and optimism is our need for a collective discussion about the state of Black America and call for a series of forums in each state. The problems and solutions we seek can only be delivered after we unitedly agree on a common course of action that we all can support with our resources and actions. For example, we all probably agree that buying and supporting Black entrepreneurs is an idea we can get behind. Let's find the other planks of our collective agreement which allow us to pursue a more prosperous future for our children. I would remiss if I did publicly announce that Jesus Christ is my Lord and Savior. This book would not be possible if I had not discovered the strength of God and his ability to make miracles happen. I hope someone reads my story and understands that you can go through despair and triumph just when you want to throw in the towel. I am convinced that believing in oneself is consistent with and strengthened by believing in God. I am ever so thankful for you taking your time to listen to the memoir of Dr. Kenneth Nolan Daniels.

SITE PLANS

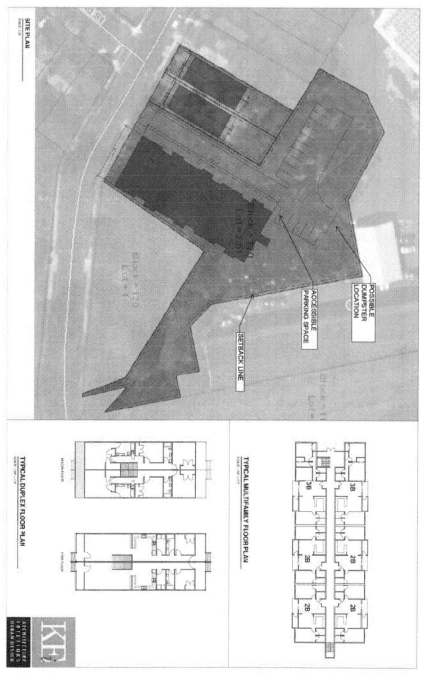

East Orange Economic Development Initiative

RUTLEDGE AVENUE CONCEPT IMAGES

AERIAL LOOKING EAST

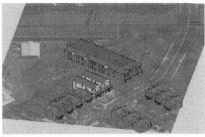

OVERVIEW OF SITE

RUTLEDGE AVENUE CONCEPT IMAGES

STREETSCAPE: RUTLEDGE AVE LOOKING EAST

STREETSCAPE: NORTH 22ND STREET LOOKING NORTH

East Orange Economic Development Initiative

December 7, 2018

Kenneth Daniels
The Daniels Center for Impact Investments and Developments
100 Park End Place
East Orange, NJ 07018

RE: *Rutledge Avenue Concept Narrative*

Mr. Daniels:

KEi Architects is pleased to submit to you this concept study for the design of multi-family residential buildings located at 156-158 Rutledge Avenue, East Orange, New Jersey.

CONCEPT

Multi-Family Building
This concept shows a 2-story structure. Each story contains 6 units for a total of 12 units. The total number is divided into 8 two-bedroom/ two-bathroom units and 4 three-bedroom/ two-bathroom units. There are two egress stairs and no elevators. There is a small lobby located on each floor closest to Rutledge Avenue. Each unit has a balcony. Utilities and bathrooms are designed to stack. The building footprint is approximately 32'-0" by 163'-0". If allowed, the building could have a third story. However, this would require discussion with the City's zoning officials. The additional units would also increase the amount of parking on the site.

We anticipate this building would be a wood framed structure with brick veneer and/ or cementitious (HardiPlank) siding. The roof would be shingled with a large roof well to locate heat pumps and other HVAC equipment as necessary. The roof well shall be a membrane roof such as Thermoplastic Olefin or Polyolefin (TPO).

Each unit consists of the following spaces: Bedrooms (2 or 3) with closets, 2 Bathrooms (1 is part of a suite), Kitchen, Dining room, Living room, and Storage/ Mechanical room. The 2 Bedroom is approximately 1,200 interior square feet and the 3 Bedroom is 1,600 interior square feet. Balconies are approximately 60 square feet.

The site would be balanced between open green space and parking. Per Section 51-164 "Off-street parking requirements," of the City of East Orange municipal code, there should be 0.5 spaces per bedroom with each dwelling unit required to have one space. The minimum number of required parking space shall be 14. The design is showing 14 plus 1 accessible space for a total of

Rutledge Avenue Development Concept Study
Page 2

15. Additional parking could be accommodated if necessary. The building is located on the site within proper setbacks. Those setbacks are being shown on the site plan.

Duplex Buildings

This concept shows 2 duplex structures, one for each lot. There will be four total units. Each unit is a 2-story three-bedroom/ three-bathroom unit. We anticipate each building would be a wood framed structure with brick veneer and/ or cementitious (HardiPlank) siding. The roof would be shingled. The building footprint, including porches, is approximately 32'-0" by 77'-0".

Each duplex unit consists of the following spaces: Bedrooms (3) with closets, 2 Bathrooms (1 is part of a suite), Kitchen, Dining room, Living room, and Storage/ Mechanical room. The Living room could be converted into a fourth bedroom if desired. The units are approximately 1,975 interior square feet. Front and rear porches are approximately 140 total square fee for each unit.

If off-street parking is provided, per Section 51-164 "Off-street parking requirements," of the City of East Orange municipal code, the minimum number of required parking space shall be 2 for each unit. The spaces could be located in the rear of the lots. Access could be created from the larger multi-family building lot. The buildings are located on the site within proper setbacks. Those setbacks are being shown on the site plan.

RISKS

We received information from the City of East Orange concerning the Rutledge Avenue Redevelopment Plan after we had completed a layout. We have attached the document to this concept study. While we feel a two- story building can match the scale of the surrounding structures. However, on page 9, the redevelopment plan document recommends that permitted structures for this property be limited to single-family detached dwellings and two-family semi-detached dwellings. On page 12 Section J, the redevelopment gives a 10-dwelling unit per acre maximum density. This may be a discussion topic with the City of East Orange.

For the duplex units, we have not provided room for driveways accessed off of Rutledge Avenue. If that is necessary and an alleyway cannot be created, the building will need to be altered to accommodate the required spaces.

If you have any questions regarding this concept, please do not hesitate to contact us.

Respectfully submitted,
KEi Architects

Lynden P. Garland, AIA
Principal

East Orange Economic Development Initiative

LAW OFFICE OF DAVID H. FAUX, P.C.
1180 AVENUE OF THE AMERICAS, 8TH FLOOR
NEW YORK, NY 10036

917-391-9468
FAX 646-654-1506

Email: davefaux@dhf-law.net
www.dhf-law.net

March 7, 2019

SENT VIA POST & WEBSITE PORTAL
The Honorable Sheila Y. Oliver
Lieutenant Governor of New Jersey
P.O. Box 001
Trenton, NJ 08625

Re: **(Re-)Naming of New Academy**

Dear Ms. Oliver,

I hope this letter finds you well. The goal of my correspondence is to cooperate in honoring Mr. Henry Daniels, hopefully through naming a school after him in northern New Jersey.

Congratulations on the recent naming of SHEILA Y. OLIVER ACADEMY. This letter is sent on behalf of my client, Professor Kenneth Daniels, who attempted to name the same school (i.e., the school replacing George Washington Carver Institute of Science and Technology at that location) after his father, Henry Daniels, the first person of color to serve as school principal in New Brunswick. This naming was part of a larger effort to strengthen education of students through The Daniels Foundation (www.thedanielsfoundation.com).

Specifically, Professor Daniels submitted a proposal to the Superintendent's office for the naming in compliance with the East Orange Board of Education Bylaws (the "Daniels Proposal"). However, the Daniels Proposal was never submitted to the BOE, having met with some irregularities prior to the December 2018 Board meeting. Furthermore, the Board violated its own bylaws by naming the school after someone still living and someone actively holding political office.

Professor Daniels asked my help on this project because he was not receiving any response from the Superintendent of the BOE. When I reached out to the Superintendent, I was referred to the Board's outside counsel at DeCotiis, Fitzpatrick & Cole, LLP. This law firm has not been responsive. As this all could be a bizarre series of miscommunications, I've reached out to you.

Both my client and I are awestruck at your community's unabashed love for you, as well as your considerable accomplishments as a public servant. You deserve an honor tantamount to the naming of a school. Still, even though you did not request this honor, it was bestowed in violation of BOE Bylaws and at the expense of a community leader who finished his path of contribution with his passing several years ago. It was hurtful that the Daniels Proposal was never considered, despite the timely and effusive efforts of my client.

Therefore, I'm wondering if you might have some sway with the officials in East Orange. The vision of you, the BOE, and Professor Daniels coming together to honor Henry Daniels will certainly leave a lasting impression of your class and humility, the community's adoration of its leaders from decades past through to present day, and a son's love for his father.

Respectfully, I will follow up this letter in a week to make sure it was properly received. My client and I both look forward to discussing all possible coordination on this project. Thank you.

Very truly yours,

LAW OFFICE OF DAVID H. FAUX, P.C.

DAVID H. FAUX

cc: Professor Kenneth Daniels (via email)

ACKNOWLEDGEMENTS

I would like to thank the following for outstanding editing and support with all remaining errors and omission solely my responsibility. Sandra L. Reid, Ph.D. for her outstanding discipline and rigor for excellence in editing the manuscript. Paije Frazier and Summer McKinney of The Paije Group for their outstanding insight and marketing of the book. Greg Schnitzler for his friendship and excellent mentorship, and Carolyn Janisé for her excellent work in the publishing of the manuscript.

I would also like to thank Gregory Schnitzler, Ronald Tillet, and Ralph Nodine for being real champions in my professional career. Neil Murphy, Carmelo Giacotto, and Francis Ahking also played a special role in my academic development, and I would be derelict not to mention their influence on me.

Also, a special note of recognition for Barry Kornblau for being a voice of reason I respected and with whom I had many enjoyable discussions and debates.

We need more champions of reason as we try to move the needle on the role of race and economics in the urban core of America.

ABOUT THE AUTHOR

DR. KENNETH N. DANIELS *also known as Dr. Kenny D* is the Founder and President of the **Daniels Foundation for Impact Investments and Development**, a non-profit organization focused on the physical and human capital of urban America with a focus on economic development. Dr. Kenneth N. Daniels was a Professor of Finance at Virginia Commonwealth University for over 30 years and has been an invited speaker at conferences such as the Institutional Investors Americas Government Funds Roundtable. Dr. Daniels has received the Sydney Futures Exchange Prize for the outstanding paper on derivatives and the outstanding paper on investments from the Eastern Finance Association.

Dr. Daniels has published over 20 referred articles in journals such as *The Journal of Money*, Credit and *Banking*, The Journal of Corporate *Finance*, *The Financial Review*, *The Journal of Financial Services Research*, *The Journal of Fixed Income*, and *The Journal of Financial Stability*. His research on municipal bonds and financial advisors has been cited in the *Dodd–Frank Wall Street Reform and Consumer Protection Act*. Dr. Daniels was a board member for the Richmond Retirement System, Virginia Community Capital Incorporated (VCC) and the Virginia Community Development Corporation (VCDC). He was also the chairman of the finance committee for the Richmond Retirement System and Virginia Community Capital. Dr. Daniels also served on the Treasury Board for the Commonwealth of Virginia from 2002 to 2010 and was a board member of the Eastern Finance Association.

Dr. Daniels is currently pursuing his second career as a writer with an emphasis on developing media content.

About the Author

Dr. Kenny D today.

LET'S STAY CONNECTED!

WEBSITE
www.daniels-foundation.org

Visit our website to learn more about the Foundation and donate to help us grow.

YOUTUBE
@The Daniels Foundation Wall of Excellence

Watch or listen to our weekly podcast LIVE every Monday 7 pm EST. It's full of easy conversations with many overcoming stories. *Like, Share and Subscribe.*

FACEBOOK – Join our online community
@TheDanielsFoundation
@kenneth.daniels.739326

INSTAGRAM
@kenneth.daniels.739326

TWITTER
@TDanielsF

EMAIL
info@daniels-foundation.org

- Become a volunteer
- Contact us for consultations regarding *Navigating through America's higher education system*
- Sign up for our newsletter and upcoming events

AMAZON
Purchase more copies of this book. For bulk orders, please contact us via email.

Made in United States
Orlando, FL
14 February 2023